WOMEN WHO SPIED

OTHER BOOKS BY A. A. HOEHLING

The Last Voyage of the *Lusitania*
The Last Train from Atlanta
They Sailed into Oblivion
A Whisper of Eternity
Lonely Command
The Fierce Lambs
The Great Epidemic
Who Destroyed the *Hindenburg?*
The Week before Pearl Harbor
The Great War at Sea

WOMEN
WHO SPIED

By A. A. HOEHLING

MADISON BOOKS

Published by Madison Books
4720 Boston Way
Lanham, Maryland 20706

First published by Dodd, Mead & Company
New York, New York

Distributed by National Book Network

The paper used in this publication meets the minimum
requirements of American National Standard for
Information Sciences—Permanence of Paper for
Printed Library Materials, ANSI Z39.48–1984. ∞™
Manufactured in the United States of America.

Library of Congress Cataloging-in-Publication Data
Hoehling, A. A. (Adolph A.)
Women who spied / A.A. Hoehling.
p.   cm.
Originally published: New York : Dodd, Mead, 1967.
Includes bibliographical references and index.
1. Military intelligence—History.   2. Women
spies—History.   I. Title.
UB270.H6   1992
355.3'432'082—dc20   92-14679 CIP

ISBN 0-8191-8486-1 (pbk. : alk. paper)

CONTENTS

Preface   vii

Acknowledgments   xi

Introduction   xv

PART ONE: DELILAH'S DISCIPLES

1. *Spy for the Continental Army*   3
   Lydia Darragh, 1777
2. *A Rainy Sunday in Greeneville*   18
   Sarah Thompson, 1864
3. *The "Alice Service"*   45
   Louise de Bettignies, 1915
4. *The Kaiser's Woman in New York*   75
   Maria de Victorica, 1918

PART TWO: WOMEN SPIES COME OF AGE

5. *Dolls in Mufti*   101
   Velvalee Dickinson, 1944
6. *Never So Few*   115
   Britain's Heroines of World War II
7. *Traitors and Crackpots*   143
   Britain's Nonheroines of World War II

8. *Spy from on High*   151
   Barbara Slade, 1943
9. *The Woman on Our Conscience*   164
   Milada Horakova, 1950

   Bibliography   193

   Index   199

PREFACE

There will be female spies as long as men remain vulnerable to the wiles of attractive, willful women. The paranoid countries in particular, such as China and the Soviet Union, are reluctant to retire this oldest of gambits in their seemingly unquenchable thirst for forbidden fruits.

Yet this personal, direct approach to the theft of other nations' secrets has become peripheral to far greater sophistication in an age of "high-tech." The term in itself is an understatement. In espionage, "high-tech" encompasses an almost infinite Pandora's box of methods and devices from spy satellites and "snooper" lasers to the tiniest of surveillance and recording instruments bearing no resemblance to old-fashioned "bugs." Voices in a room, for example, can be picked up even from imperceptible vibrations through window glass.

The United States pioneered its "spy-in-the-sky" in 1961 with the launching of SAMOS, or "satellite and mission observation system." The remarkable five-ton space vehicle automatically developed photographs taken by its ultra long range cameras. It made obsolete high-flying spy planes such as the U-2, or the "Black Bird."

Since then, all the major powers have rocketed similar satellites into orbit. Military or industrial secrets have become quite naked to these stratospheric Peeping Toms which are said to be able to identify people on the ground below, determine if a factory is in production, wholly or partially, or even to spot a submerged submarine. Optical satellites snap thousands of photographs, then parachute the film to ground stations or to aircraft with special retrieving gear.

Why bother to attempt to steal plans for a potential adversary's new missile frigate, say, when its progress in the shipyard can be photographed on a daily basis?

Greatly advanced spy satellites eliminated much of the guesswork out of planning for the Persian Gulf War, then provided daily overviews of the conflict's progress.

Thus far, the satellites have proven invulnerable to destruction or other counter-measures. Unlike their human counterparts, these "secret agents" cannot be compromised, arrested or disposed of by a firing squad.

By far the most costly espionage operation since World War II was "Jennifer," involving a 51,000-ton vessel, the *Hughes Glomar Explorer.*

In 1968, Navy sonar monitors in Hawaii, routinely tracking Soviet ships, recorded a diesel-powered submarine of the Golf II class abruptly disappearing from their screens. At the same time sonobuoys, which the Navy had "sown" throughout the Pacific, relayed several explosions—then silence. The position was some 750 miles northwest of Honolulu.

Washington was not much interested in this semi-obsolete warship, although it was known to be armed with three nuclear-warhead missiles and "low-yield" nuclear torpedoes. But it obviously carried code books, encrypting and decrypting machines, quite essential to the breaking of Russian naval codes. This appeared to offer an opportunity to harvest an intelligence treasure even though the lost submersible was in waters over three miles deep.

Six years later, the CIA had created, with the assistance of Howard Hughes and the Sun Shipbuilding and Drydock Co., the monster *Explorer* or "Jennifer," that was distinguished by a towering derrick amidships and complex grappling equipment. The price tag totaled more than one-half billion and involved at least 4,000 personnel, both men and women.

What happened after the strange vessel arrived over the sunken submarine remains something of a mystery that only the CIA can unravel. Its official version, doubtlessly leaked, was that "Jennifer" was largely a failure. The submarine had supposedly broken up in the lifting process and only a handwritten "journal" had been recovered from that small section of the submarine that had been salvaged. If, indeed, the entire vessel, its codes, coding machines and missiles had been recovered, would the CIA, scarcely a talkative agency, ever have said so? Certainly no photographs of what might have been exhumed from the deep were ever released.

International intelligence and counter-intelligence have become big business. Since they are invariably government sponsored, the craft is another huge bureaucracy. No one knows how many millions are employed in the fiercely guarded warrens of espionage in Washington, Moscow, Peking or throughout the world. How great is the CIA's payroll, or how many are employed in the armed forces' far-reaching intelligence network?

As in more conventional offices, women play a major role, from simple filing and bookkeeping, to advanced computer interpretation and photo analysis. Yesterday's cloak-and-dagger it surely is not. Tedium has replaced what might once have been considered glamor. Yet the missions and the goals remain unchanged.

ACKNOWLEDGMENTS

There are many to whom the author owes a debt of gratitude for their invaluable assistance in making this book possible. Risking the inherent danger of omitting unintentionally some names, I would nonethelesss like to make a matter of record the aid in research or "leads" in the quest for factual grist provided by those whose names follow.

Starting first with the final chapter, "The Woman on Our Conscience," I should note that for nearly twelve years I have been attempting to reassemble the shattered biographical threads of the life of Milada Horakova, who I believe places with Edith Cavell and other martyred heroines of all time. Her story is more than a personal tragedy, profound as it is. It is the story of a continuing struggle in our lifetime of primordial force attempting to snuff out man's birthright of freedom and to erase the gains of civilization over the centuries.

Two Czechoslovakians in particular, both residents of Washington, D.C., Dr. Petr Zenkl and Dr. Bohuslav Horak, have been tireless in their efforts to reconstruct for the author the life of Milada and also to present in all of its frightening detail the death writhings of the Czech Republic. The experience, even at this distance, has been much like watching some deadly bacteria multiply under the microscope, with the added horror that there is no positive vaccine against these bacteria and that, quite possibly, they can all surge from their glass slides and test tubes and, silently, infest the viewer at will.

Mrs. Rose Pelantova also assisted me with her own memories. I was fortunate enough to interview her in her New York apartment shortly before her death in 1959.

In addition to those mentioned in the chapter, these other friends of Milada's, through her husband or Zenkl, have helped with their reminiscences: Jaromina Batkova-Zackova, Vladimir Krajina, Josef Sevcik, Jaroslav Stransky, Cenek Thorn and Dr. Alice Masarykova.

The International League for the Rights of Man, various European "captive nations" committees working in this country, and Radio Free Europe also searched their files for such information as they possessed for this chapter.

Many responded as well in the call for help during the research on "Britain's Heroine of World War II." They include Miss Vera Atkins, a director of SOE, in London; E. J. Clark, Assistant Adjutant, Women's Transport Service (FANY); Rose Coombs, Librarian, Imperial War Museum, London; John Coote, Exmouth, England, formerly of Scotland Yard; Mrs. Odette Hallowes; Lieutenant Commander P. K. Kemp, Naval Historical Branch, Ministry of Defense, London; D. W. King, Chief Librarian, Ministry of Defense; Countess Roberta de Mauduit, Plourivo, France; H. G. Pearson, Home Office, Whitehall, London; and Mrs. Virginia R. Stuart, Washington; also these authors: Jean Overton Fuller, London; R. J. Minney, London; Leslie Reade, London; and Mrs. Elizabeth P. MacDonald McIntosh, Leesburg, Virginia, who was with the OSS; and Edward H. Cookridge, London.

Mrs. Barbara Wheeler, Miss Constance Babington-Smith and Robert Bulmer, all of England, made possible the aerial snooping chapter. Photo reconnaissance, whether from low-flying aircraft or high-orbiting satellites, has become an increasingly important, as well as scientific, part of national defense.

Richard J. Heaney, Bureau of Prisons, U.S. Department of Justice, H. P. Leinbaugh, of the Federal Bureau of Investigation, together with a considerable number of persons from her two principal New York neighborhoods should be credited for their aid in trying to unravel the several mysteries of the "doll spy," Velvalee Dickinson.

For information before World War II, pertinent or lucid living memory is becoming increasingly rare. However, Mrs. Edna Yardley, the widow of Herbert Yardley, both parent and author of "The American Black Chamber," helped to resolve some of the riddles and confirm other facts about Mme. Victorica, the most colorful spy in America in 1918. George V. Nolan, Gate of Heaven Cemetery, Hawthorne, Westchester County, New York, confirmed that Maria Victorica is actually buried there; in the early stages of my research, with professional cynicism, I entertained doubts as to such a person's existence.

Mrs. Virginia R. Gray, Duke University Library, Durham, North Carolina, deserves the credit for "discovering" Sarah Thompson, General Morgan's nemesis. She informed me of a rare manuscript collection. Miss Ruth Bergling, of Washington and Mrs. Cyrus Morris, of Chevy Chase, Maryland, descendants of Sarah, substantiated the documents and added from the storehouse of their own memories. Mrs. Sarajane Goodman, Tennessee State Library and Archives, Mrs. Alexandra Lee Levin, Baltimore, and Mrs. Alene Lowe White, Librarian, Western Reserve Historical Society, Cleveland, also assisted in this chapter on Civil War cloak-and-dagger.

As for the Revolution, it is not even easy to find descendants. However, much of what little is to be found confirming the existence and deeds of Lydia Darragh is in the Historical Society of Pennsylvania, Philadelphia, well catalogued by the capable Executive Director, Henry Cadwalader.

Of general advisory assistance were Brigadier General Thomas J. Betts, ret., of Washington, a veteran G-2 officer, Stanley P. Lovell, of Watertown, Massachusetts, formerly of the OSS; and Colonel Allison Ind, ret., now of Southampton, England, a well-known author on espionage, and a fair hand once himself.

A word on periodicals and newspapers: General background material or confirmatory evidence for chapters going back through but not beyond World War II was found in literally hundreds of newspapers in this country and overseas, as well as in magazines, most of them still of familiarity and too obvious to demand listing.

Earlier than the present century, the daily press becomes quite meager as a substantiating source, and almost totally worthless at the time of the Revolution. Even original manuscripts have at least an implausible, if not often incoherent, quality.

However, these specific periodicals contain the only known source material on Lydia Darragh: *American Quarterly Review,* 1827; *Bulletin of the Historical Society of Pennsylvania,* Vol. I; *Philadelphia Historical Bulletin,* 1917, and *St. Nicholas Magazine,* February, 1898 ("How a Woman Saved an Army," by H. A. Ogden.)

The *Tennessee Historical Society Quarterly,* Vol. 19, contains material on General Morgan's death.

The *American Magazine,* June, 1929, contains an article on Leonie Van Houtte in Lille's "Alice Service."

The facilities of these libraries were used: the Army Library, the Pentagon; the District of Columbia Public Library; the Library of Congress; the National Archives; the Navy Library; the New York Public Library. Source material reference was kindly sent by Miss Jane Gwynn, Reading Room, the British Museum, London.

And last, but surely not least, Mr. Allen Klots, Jr., editor of Dodd, Mead, whose idea this book was in the first place.

INTRODUCTION

Almost any of them might have passed for the girl or the woman next door—except for one unique characteristic which set each apart. She was a spy.

These women adopted an unfamiliar profession, secretive in the ultimate, from motives as varied as their feminine whims or wiles: patriotism, a love of adventure, revenge, or merely because fate swept them into it. Almost none did so for the money. And in the few instances where funds *did* change hands, the ladies were scandalously underpaid.

Cloak-and-dagger provided escape from the humdrum and boredom. It was an intoxicant, reprieving the fairer sex from the kitchen and laundry and from all the tedium of a woman's lot—then.

They were nobodies who often became instant some-bodies, even though their neighborhoods were rarely aware of the metamorphosis. And that was the way it was supposed to be. What mattered: they were at least important to them-selves.

Lives that had dragged along an unrelievedly gray canvas blossomed into the iridescent hues of the full spectrum. Existence was exhilarating. Wits, dulled from the most mundane of household challenges, were sharpened and marched off to war, double-time. They relied on those wits to keep alive. Theirs was the reward of self-satisfaction, of a frontline intimacy of participation.

And, insofar as recorded history attests, it began with Delilah; the seductive hireling of the Philistines launched coming generations of women in the profession of espionage. The famous Biblical tribe had reasoned with an animal-like canniness when they sent Delilah to compromise their archenemy and mighty Hebrew leader, Samson. He could not resist her allure. He whispered to her the secret of his great strength—his hair. And thereupon she cut it off. Any school boy or girl knows what happened next. . . .

From out of the same limbo of centuries there was also Theodora, who entertained her Byzantine court with naked dances. She was a lascivious, despotic empress who employed spies of her own sex to ferret out intrigue and meet it with counterintrigue. Theodora's methods, if unorthodox and in some respects ahead of her times, totaled up nonetheless to an effective reign.

In the sixteenth century, the ever suspicious Queen Elizabeth elevated cloak-and-daggery to a science through her "master spy," Sir Francis Walsingham, coached in subterfuge by the Jesuits as well as blatant nonclerics in Italy.

This most effective Secretary of State gathered evidence through spies and intercepted mail which sent Elizabeth's own cousin, Mary Queen of Scots, to the beheading block. But Walsingham's domestic espionage was but a fraction of his furtive portfolio. He created listening posts throughout the civilized world, and in parts of the uncivilized.

It was Walsingham who, at the Queen's inspiration, laid

foundations for the future role of a nation's embassies. They would become not alone foreign extensions of goodwill but —perhaps more so than not—vipers' nests of snooping.

Queen Elizabeth's court spawned the predecessor of the "cultural attaché," whose increasingly important role would be that of rearranger and, if possible, wrecker in a "friendly" nation whose government was nonetheless not quite friendly enough.

Walsingham's tour de force, after disposing of the Queen of Scots, came the next year, in 1588, when he warned of the aggressive preparations of the Spanish Armada. Agents in the house of the grand Admiral Don Alvarez de Bazan, re-layed hints back to London. They proved well-founded hints.

It was perhaps no coincidence that the sixty-two-year-old admiral dropped dead on February 9, just before the great armada sailed to its defeat. Spain, overnight deprived of her greatest naval tactician, had gone into battle at a distinct disadvantage against adversaries of the caliber of Drake, Hawkins and Frobisher.

Many of Walsingham's innovations remain gospel in the ever enlarging, ever adapting bible of espionage. He never, for example, employed the same agent too long. The learned Sir Francis, who spoke half a dozen languages, understood the perils to employers of the double agent. At the same time he established the Janus character of the tourist, even though the camera and the collapsible binocular would have to await another century. Through Walsingham, Queen Elizabeth became a regal patron to all future spies.

Two centuries later, Karl Schulmeister proved a worthy successor to Walsingham. Napoleon Bonaparte's cloak-and-dagger chief was not averse to paying women, whether of court or courtesan stature, for information. He scored his greatest coup by causing the Duc d'Enghien's mistress to be an unwitting femme fatale. In 1804, the Duke, as a leader of the exiled Bourbons, posed the only palpable threat to the self-proclaimed Emperor.

Schulmeister kidnapped the girl and brought her to a château in southern Alsace, near the frontier. He then forged a letter for help, in which "she" assured her lover that he could bribe the jailors and then dash with her to safety.

The counterfeiting was perfect. The Prince, just as in the fairy tales, responded to the rescue of fair lady. Napoleon's border guards seized the Duke several miles short of his goal, and he was sentenced to death.

As a final indignity, the execution squad, assembled at night, made the condemned hold aloft the lantern, by the yellow glow of which they aimed at his heart. His hand was steady. The riflemen did not miss.

A man, whether spy or soldier in uniform, was far from a preferred insurance risk in wartime. It was different with the fairer sex, much different. Gallantry persisted into and throughout the nineteenth century.

Women, caught up to the elbows in the cookie jar of espionage, became the objects of solicitous pardon. Their captors lacked only a deep bow and the sweep of a feathered hat to lend a final flourish to their all-forgiving nature. If the females were imprisoned, it was rarely for long—for, after all, girls would be girls, wouldn't they?

In the case of one otherwise obscure suspected agent for the Confederacy, Christine Ford, the jail door in Washington just "happened" to be left unlocked one night. Although this gambit had been employed before to rid commanding officers of embarrassing charges and obligations, the aided escape of Miss Ford was garnished with especial éclat. It was believed that President Lincoln himself had given the extralegal order.

He did not trust his fire-breathing Secretary of War Edwin Stanton. Suppose the latter had ordered a woman to be executed? To the Great Emancipator this possibility was worse than unthinkable.

The global-scale conflicts of the twentieth century brought a cold brutality to espionage. Skirts, tresses, or a pretty face were not enough to stay a firing squad, the hangman, or, in Nazi Germany, the headsman's ax.

Women spies faced their Maker along with their male comrades-in-arms. Death stole beside them as an unwelcome but nonetheless constant companion. They died in lonely horror, these women of iron nerves who defied the enemy in a contest which had ceased to recognize any rules of warfare, and no longer was tempered by old-fashioned notions of chivalry.

Armed conflict, especially the science of espionage, became as impersonal as an electronic computer—a robot which as a matter of fact is assuming many of the old memory and deductive prerogatives of secret agents.

If mercy glimmered through, it was by chance, not intent. War no longer in its essence was fun, an adventure, or an exciting demimonde.

. . . This is the story of several women spies. It is not offered as an encyclopedia, an anthology, or a book of oft-told tales. It *is* an attempt to fill in some gaps on the shelves of espionage, to give credit where credit has been overlooked, and to present in fuller, truer dimension what has been obscured or garishly colored through the often clumsy brushstrokes of recall.

ILLUSTRATIONS

Following page 78

Lydia Darragh
The Loxley House
General John Hunt Morgan
Belle Boyd
Sarah Thompson
Sarah Thompson's Dismissal
World War I Poster
French Hostages at Lille
Louise de Bettignies
Notice of Execution of Civilians
Identity Card
The Kodak Girls
I. D. Card of Violette Szabo
Diana Rowden
Vera Leigh
Noor Inayat Khan
Odette Hallowes
Barbara Slade
A Belhamelin-Type Site
A "Diver" Site
Milada Horakava

Part 1

DELILAH'S DISCIPLES

". . . women are as brave and responsible as men, often more so. They are entitled to a share in the defense of their beliefs no less than men."

—Maurice Buckmaster

1

❖

SPY FOR THE CONTINENTAL ARMY

➻ *Lydia Darragh, 1777*

George Washington learned the value of women spies early in America's history. In fact, although there is no evidence that he was a student of Walsingham or of others who followed him, Washington gave serious heed to the daily gleanings from a considerable number of spies, largely amateur, who worked for the Continental Army.

Not all were successful. The most tragic example was Nathan Hale, the heroic Connecticut schoolteacher. His failure as a courier that September, 1776, led to his hanging. But he taught future generations how to die.

In December of the same year, John Honeyman, a butcher who lived on the road from Trenton to Princeton, was eminently more successful. While encouraging his neighbors to think he was in the pay of the British, or even a double agent, Honeyman carried the word to Washington at Valley Forge that the Hessian garrisons in his two neighboring towns were drunk and lethargic from too much Christmas season revelry. The result was dramatic victories, first at

Trenton, next at Princeton.*

Although General Washington did not possess the reserves to hold either prize, the success was like an injection of adrenaline to morale after the recent loss of Long Island and forts along the Hudson Palisades, the last toehold on Manhattan Island, together with the defeat at White Plains.

Then in August and October, 1777, came the brilliant victories of Bennington and Saratoga respectively, climaxing the starting months of the third year of the Revolution. At the latter, General John Burgoyne surrendered an army of nearly 6,000 men with 42 cannon and full equipment to General Horatio Gates.

However, there was no time or even full occasion for rejoicing. In between these twin triumphs, Sir William Howe marched into Philadelphia and hung out his "at home" sign. The English commander actually liked the colonists. However, Philadelphia was where all that "trouble" started, and to George III, a ruler noted for neither foresight nor common sense, the image of the Union Jack flying before Independence Hall was a warming one.

Commencing his second winter amidst the winds and snowdrifts of the Valley Forge area, General Washington maintained surprising optimism about maintaining the offensive in the face of continuing privation and dissent in the ranks.

Even as the snowflakes slanted across the dead stubble of the Pennsylvania fields, the Commander-in-Chief was asking his generals if they would recommend a winter campaign, with Philadelphia its prize.

---

* Undoubtedly there were true double agents in the Revolution. One was a somewhat shadowy figure, Ann Bates, who flitted back and forth between the lines, ultimately marrying a British officer and sailing to sanctuary in England.

The Marquis de Lafayette counseled what seemed obvious: give the men "a good rest in winter quarters." General Nathaniel Greene suggested any operations at this time would be "very precurious." Major General John Sullivan and others contented themselves with lengthy analyses of relative strengths of the opposing forces, in men and equipment.

Estimates of the British forces in the Philadelphia theater ranged from 6,000 all the way up to 15,000. Actually, Howe's army was not markedly larger than Washington's—then mustering approximately 11,000 effectives.

Winter in 1777, even as in 1776, did not present an auspicious setting for any offensive. Bothering Washington, nonetheless, was the suspicion that his adversary would not be wholly adverse to moving troops and mounting an attack in snow and blow-freezing temperatures. Lord Howe's troops were equipped with fine rifles and artillery, warm clothing from Yorkshire's best woolen mills, and their stomachs were always filled. The British should have been able to fight at any time.

General Washington therefore had to keep abreast of Howe's intentions. As a professional engineer, the canny leader of the Patriots held no brief for guesswork. He already possessed his own intelligence service—an ancestral "G-2." It was headed by Colonel Elias Boudinot, a distinguished patriot and statesman.

The network which he spun and then endeavored, as chief spider, to dominate, was at best loose, amateurish, and operated on a catch-as-catch-can basis of expediency. It comprised farmers, merchants, itinerant artisans, country girls selling produce, almost anyone who could enter enemy-held territory unobtrusively and return with tidbits of military information.

When Philadelphia fell after the disasters of Brandywine and Germantown in September, Boudinot set up listening posts on a wide semicircle from Red Lyon, near Chester, Pennsylvania, thirteen miles south of Philadelphia, all along the western perimeter of the occupied city to Frankford, on the northeast. Boudinot, who himself explained only that he "managed the intelligence of the Army," usually met with his agents at the Rising Sun Tavern, two miles west of Frankford and six miles north of the center of Philadelphia. In turn, the tavern rendezvous was handy to Washington's headquarters at Whitemarsh, close to Norristown and twelve miles northwest of the city. It was slightly advanced eastward from his previous Valley Forge encampment.

Boudinot entrusted the Red Lyon intelligence to Major John Clark, Jr., an imaginative young officer whose daily diary entries commenced with the preface:

"Sent in a spy today . . ."

He wanted to obtain information on arrival of reinforcements, changes of bivouacs, assemblage of wagons and other heavy equipment, even the moving of a gun emplacement. All of these chips fitted into the mosaic of the enemy's intentions, so important in the deliberations of General Washington.

During the last days of November and the first few of December, it became obvious from Major Clark's reports that the British were "in motion" within their broad Philadelphia base. This did not necessarily mean that they were on the march. But it was obvious to Clark and to his superior, Boudinot, that troops were being equipped and provisioned for something quite more than drills or even maneuvers.

What was going to happen? And when?

George Washington was sufficiently concerned to order 1,200 Rhode Island troops and 1,000 more from Virginia, Maryland, and Pennsylvania into his foremost breastworks, facing Chestnut Hill. Now he could do no more than bide his time until he obtained a better idea of the direction and strength of the possible thrust.

He could not have expected that the clinching information would emanate from a Quaker household—that of the William Darraghs on 177 South Second Street, near Spruce, in Philadelphia. Known as the "Loxley House," the comfortably appointed structure was situated across from the more sumptuous residence of Captain John Cadwalader. This farsighted patriot had used the street for drilling his "silk stocking" company of Pennsylvania militia.

General Howe himself had headquartered for a time in the Cadwalader home. Although he had requisitioned Darragh's house as a spillover for his staff, he yielded to the entreaties of both William and his slight, inconspicuous-appearing wife, Lydia. The British commander agreed to use only the parlor as a "council chamber" for staff meetings.

Lydia would never have been mistaken for a spy. She was the antithesis of Delilah, in fact or fiction. Nature had not complicated her existence with feminine beauty. However, what she lacked in ostentation or sex appeal, she amply compensated for in loyalty and quiet daring, as an opportunist and improviser.

For some weeks, Lydia had been transmitting morsels of what was going on in the occupied city to her oldest son, Lieutenant Charles Darragh, in Washington's army, via her youngest, John, who was fourteen. She reasoned that the youth was as innocent-appearing a courier as an agent could desire.

The enemy's irresolution in not commandeering the Darragh home in the first place was next compounded by his underestimation of its mistress. During the afternoon of December 2 it became apparent that an unusually important conference was to be held in the parlor. An officer notified Lydia that the General had suggested the family retire early, "as they wished to use the room that night free from interruption."

It was a singularly naïve request, in that it aroused the suspicions of Mrs. Darragh. The officer might as well have told her that the British were contemplating a surprise attack on the Continental Army.

Lydia obediently went to bed. But she could not sleep. As she would recall in a letter, "a presentiment of evil" weighed upon her spirits.

Finally, she could contain her curiosity no longer. She threw back the covers, quickly slipped a dressing gown over her shoulders and tiptoed, barefooted, out of her bedroom, into the hall and down the unlighted stairway, step by step. Every squeaking of the boards, it seemed, would betray her.

However, she gained the keyhole of the parlor door a few minutes before Lord Howe's officers completed their meeting. She was in time to overhear the conference's conclusion: the British would march out of Philadelphia by night, December 4, and let loose what they hoped would be a knockout punch at General Washington's "unprepared condition." She also heard a few of the figures pertaining to the strength of the attacking forces.

She hurried upstairs, and was in bed barely in time to hear a thump-thump up the stairs, then knocks on her door. She remained silent, wondering. Then, the knocks ceased.

In her feeling of guilt, Lydia did not guess the obvious—that the British officer had come only to ask her to lock up, blow out the remaining candles, and douse any coals that glowed in the grate. She waited until his receding footsteps faded along the short corridor, then down the stairs into silence. Lydia's fears were eased. But she could not sleep.

How, she kept asking herself, could she relay to George Washington the intentions of the British? She could not conceive of a logical pretext for sending her younger son, once more, through the lines. Besides, time was short. Lydia became convinced that she and she alone must bear the responsibility of passing into American lines. Once the question was resolved, her method seemed to her obvious.

She would take a sack to the Frankford mill, for flour. Five miles northeast of the city, it lay on the route to Whitemarsh and was not too much of a walk, even for a middle-aged little lady in wintertime.

Other women, widowed or alone while their husbands fought in the army, made this trip to the mill with regularity. Like them, Lydia possessed a British pass to leave the city limits. The occupation forces had to consider food an absolute necessity.

The Quaker wife did not confide in her husband—not necessarily that she may have distrusted him, but because she was a sufficiently canny disciple of Delilah's to be aware of the perils inherent in alerting too many people to any mission. Curiously, William Darragh's only surprise and concern were in her refusal to allow her maid to accompany her. Lydia was politely adamant. Her husband remonstrated in vain.

Sack in hand, that Wednesday, December 3, in her poke

bonnet and plain, ankle-length gray dress which showed that she was a Quaker, Lydia Darragh walked at a brisk clip through the frozen streets and lanes of Philadelphia.

Sentries scarcely bothered to notice, much less challenge this inconspicuous figure.

Meanwhile, Washington's patrols realized that something was up. Major Clark started a messenger toward headquarters with the intelligence that the British might be preparing an offensive. But, if so, when and where? Or was this just the incessant maneuvering and changing of regiments which were so characteristic of a large European army?

Another valuable officer, Captain Allen McLane, who was leading his one hundred hard-riding cavalrymen up and down icy, rutted paths west of the city, in the vicinity of Chestnut Hill, tried to find some hint of "motion" in that sector. It was approximately three miles in advance of the Continental Army's right wing.

McLane operated with small units in unexpected places. On a small scale, he was perhaps pioneer of the surprise and blitz technique. Once, for example, accompanied by only two or three equally daring tough officers, he smashed into a formal reception in honor of Lord Howe himself. The swashbuckling cavalrymen shot up the chandeliers, killed the Hussian guard, then remounted their horses and were away almost before the British could comprehend what had happened. Even if the military toll were not great, the party, certainly, was ruined.

Lydia arrived in the early afternoon in Frankford—a sort of no-man's-land of the Revolution* lightly held by the pa-

---

* Frankford's growing pains were not easy. Shortly after the war, a traveler wrote of "its mud and wretchedness, its barking dogs and squalling babies where society seems in a transition state from filth to cleanliness and consequently from vice to Godliness."

triots. The Queen's Rangers had attempted only the month before to raid the post and take prisoners but were repulsed with losses.

She did not loiter at the mill on Frankford Creek. She asked the miller to fill her sack, promising to be back shortly. Lydia then walked westward along Nice Town Lane toward the Rising Sun Tavern. Shortly before reaching it, Lydia was at long last challenged. It turned out, by coincidence, that her challenger was a family acquaintance, Lieutenant Colonel Thomas Craig, of the Third Pennsylvania "Mounted," popular units in the Continental Army, not quite infantry, hardly cavalry.

Craig walked beside his friend, who cautiously at first explained she was merely trying to visit her son. Then, she confided in him what she had overheard. The officer listened with interest, then suggested that she must be weary. She was.

He left her in a nearby farmhouse, asking the owners to give her supper. Then he rode off, possibly to convey Lydia Darragh's tale to headquarters. Apparently Lydia herself was not wholly certain that he would do so. And if he did, would he relay the word in time?

Still unsatisfied, Lydia hurried through her light meal and then continued by foot on the now dark, increasingly cold road toward the Rising Sun Tavern, where she had the good fortune apparently to meet Colonel Boudinot in person.

He reported in his journals,* "after dinner a little poor looking insignificant old woman came in and solicited leave

---

* These journals, published in 1894, did not identify the Quaker woman by name, but the pages dealing with the tavern incident do, curiously, use her name in the chapter heading. This suggests that the name may have been in his original manuscript. As President of Congress after the Revolution, Boudinot signed the Treaty of Peace with England.

to go into the country to buy some flour. While we were asking some questions she walked up to me and put into my hands a dirty old needlework with various small pockets in it. Surprised at this, I told her to return, she should have an answer."

The Colonel opened up the needlework to find several small pockets sewed inside. From one he removed a piece of paper rolled "into the form of a pipe shank." On the paper was fairly legible writing which revealed that Howe was coming out of the city with 5,999 men, 13 pieces of cannon, baggage wagons and 11 boats on wagon wheels (a kind of pioneering amphibious vehicle).

When Boudinot compared this "with other information" in his possession, he decided it was correct. At once he rode to Whitemarsh and conveyed to Washington personally "the naked facts without comment or opinion," as they were secreted in the needlework.

After the General had "received it with much thoughtfulness," the Colonel presented his own theory: that Howe would cross the Delaware under the pretense of marching to New York, but instead recross the river above Bristol, just north of Philadelphia, and hit the Americans from the rear, which was vulnerable.

"Deep in thought," George Washington did not utter "a single observation." Not a little frustrated at his commander's sphinxlike attitude, Boudinot repeated, "earnestly," everything he had said.

Finally, in terse words, Washington said he did not think Howe was going to cross the river, that he was carrying along the boats only as a "deception." Instead, he was certain the enemy would take a "Bye Road" and attack his army's left wing, rather than the rear.

Boudinot was to admit that he thought "the Old Fox," as

Washington was often dubbed with affection, was not in this judgment so foxy. He was to confide to his diary that the General was reasoning "under a manifest mistake."

A late dispatch from Major Clark arrived about this time, giving the alarm that the British were truly "in motion," moving out of Philadelphia with "a number of flat-bottomed boats and carriages and scantlings [pieces of cut timber presumably for road surfacing or bridge building]and are busy pressing horses and wagons. No persons permitted to come out...."

The dashing cavalry captain, Allen McLane, sent an even more urgent warning before midnight. His scouts cantering along the Skipjack Road, near Schuylkill River, had made out shielded lanterns approaching at a distance which hinted of an army's advance units. McLane predicted without qualification that "an attempt to surprise the American camp at Whitemarsh was about to be made."

At 3:00 A.M., Thursday, December 4, Howe's patrols opened fire on the Continental's front lines, and from a byroad as Washington had predicted. For the remainder of the early morning hours, Howe's Redcoats dug into positions along a ridge beyond Chestnut Hill, facing principally the American right, rather than the left flank as the American commander had theorized. However, what mainly mattered: the Patriots were ready. The surprise had been total failure.

"Having now so respectable a force in the field," wrote Major Benjamin Tallmadge, of Long Island, commanding the Second Regiment, Light Dragoons, "and especially the Northern Army being flushed with recent victory and hoping that the other troops would vie with them in the contest, a battle was rather desired than avoided.

"After continuing several days in his first position, by daybreak on the 7th General Howe took a new position in front of our left wing, on the flank of which I was posted with a body of horse, together with [Colonel Daniel] Morgan's* Light Infantry and Riflemen. We came into contact with the British Light Infantry and Dragoons in which Major [Joseph] Morris of our infantry was killed [one of twenty-seven American casualties].

"I thought a general battle inevitable, but neither general thought it prudent to descend into the plain. After continuing in this position a few days, General Howe retired to Philadelphia for winter quarters to our great surprise."

Howe subsequently contented himself with a brief explanation: ". . . the enemy's camp being as strong on their center and left as upon the right, their seeming determination to hold this position; and unwilling to expose the troops longer to the weather in this inclement season, without tents or baggage of any kind . . . I returned on the 8th."

Lydia Darragh returned to the farmhouse of her benefactor near the Rising Sun Tavern, and doubtlessly waited there until the roads cleared of military traffic. When once more in the sanctuary of 177 South Second Street, she was paid a visit by a very puzzled British officer.

"I know," he conceded, alluding to the council meeting the night of December 2, "that you were asleep for I knocked at your chamber door three times before you heard me. I am entirely at a loss to imagine who gave General Washington information of our intended attack—unless the walls of the house could speak?

"When we arrived near Whitemarsh we found all their

---

* The famous Morgan had already figured prominently in the expedition against Canada, and at Saratoga would acquire new laurels in January, 1781, at the victory of Cowpens, Carolina.

cannon mounted and the troops prepared to receive us. And we have marched back like a parcel of fools."

General Washington, in his report to Congress, mentioned merely, "in the course of last week from a variety of intelligence I had reason to expect that General Howe was preparing to give us a general action."

The Commander-in-Chief expressed, in an order to the army, his "warmest thanks to Colonel Morgan and the officers and men of his intrepid corps for their gallant behavior in the several skirmishes with the enemy yesterday. He hopes the most spirited conduct will distinguish the whole army and gain them a just title to the praise of their country and the glory due brave men."

Another senior American officer was somewhat more succinct in summing up Morgan's role: he "messed up" the British.

Washington made no mention of Lydia Darragh. For that matter, in all of his journals, reports, and orders credit or even passing references to women are conspicuously absent. Conceivably, he shared a prevalent prejudice against the opposite sex's being identified with duties other than child-bearing or housekeeping. Spying? It was scarcely feminine.

However, Tallmadge (who lived into his eighty-second year) was less reluctant to accord mention when such was indicated. Noting subsequent minor operations in Pennsylvania, Tallmadge referred to his questioning of a "country girl with eggs" coming back from the city.

And while this "young female" was volunteering information, an enemy patrol opened fire. Gallantly, Tallmadge set her up on his horse and together they galloped away, in a whirlwind of "considerable firing of pistols and not a little wheeling and charging." However, like all the iron-nerved heroines in storybooks, "she remained unmoved and never once complained of fear after she mounted my horse."

Every intent of a thoroughly dispirited Lord Howe continued to be conveyed with incredible speed to Valley Forge, to which Washington's army had now retired. The British commanding general could not outwit Boudinot's spy "management" and plucky agents such as Lydia Darragh or country girls with their baskets.

It turned out that this passive commander had asked for transfer home at the time of Burgoyne's surrender. In February, 1778, his request was granted, and the often querulous Sir Henry Clinton replaced him.

On June 18, the enemy marched out of Philadelphia, after arranging for 3,000 Tories to sail down the Delaware River aboard Royal Navy vessels, which had been under the command of Howe's brother, Admiral Richard Howe.

Not all of the Tories elected to go. Peggy Shippen, in her teens, for one, whose beauty and personal charm had earned her the title of "reigning belle" of Philadelphia society, stayed. Who could be cross with one so lovely? Certainly not the handsome and hitherto brave Major General Benedict Arnold. The Connecticut-born officer, who was a recent widower, married Peggy while he was military governor of Philadelphia—and compromised her in his plot to seize West Point, using her as a secretary in his coded correspondence with Clinton. (She followed him into what amounted to his exile in disgrace in England.)

A few Quakers had cooperated with the occupation forces. Two of them, convicted of leading British patrols against an American outpost, were hung after Philadelphia was returned to its original government.

Lydia herself went strangely unrewarded for her busy and daring mission that December night, 1777. In fact, the Friends Society subsequently decided that she and her husband, William and—certainly!—her son who had served in the army had been altogether too martial for a peace-loving religious group. So the three were expelled from membership. The young boy, John, as an adolescent, was afforded opportunity to redeem himself.

And Lydia, an obscure, imperfectly documented figure at best, faded into the peculiarly lonely oblivion of spies who have risen to unusual demands of the moment, then vanished into the wings without so much as a bow.

2

⁝

A RAINY SUNDAY IN GREENEVILLE

⟶ Sarah Thompson, 1864

The art of espionage did not progress in the nineteenth century far beyond its simple antecedents of the Revolution. But women in the Civil War responded in unprecedented numbers to their own urges to make some contribution to the great struggle.

Nurses, housewives, many others left alone when husbands, fathers, or brothers shouldered rifles and said "good-bye!" stumbled sooner or later into tidbits they considered of explosive value. And they could not rest until they conveyed their trove through the lines.

In their enthusiasm and magnificent unfamiliarity with things martial, they deluged Union and Confederate headquarters alike with a magpie's outpourings of gossip, trivia, the shadows, at best, cast by more substantial images.

Some, the girls, went so far as to masquerade as men. They succeeded in enlisting and donning the blue or gray. But in the rough-tough male world of camp and barracks, this play-acting could not long continue undetected.

One slight, attractive Canadian girl, however, proved a rule's exception. Sarah Emma Edmonds survived the war with a Michigan regiment. Sometimes she was "Private Thompson," sometimes a spy, finally a nurse. For three adventurous years she concealed her identity from the majority of her colleagues.

The cloak-and-dagger profession, far from a science, at least broadened out from the exclusive province of the court, keyholes, and back-fence whisperings. The era of the amateur spy, in significant quantities, had dawned.

A very few names of the mob of female agents and would-be agents emerged as legends. Much of their narrative could as well have come from the dossier of a Baron Munchausen. On the other hand, there was fact among the fiction.

Belle Boyd, a tall, eighteen-year-old Martinsburg, West Virginia, brunette in 1861, was destined to become the best-known skirted spy of the Civil War. Her usefulness, however, was considerably impaired by the inordinate amount of time spent in Federal military prisons from New York to Fortress Monroe, Virginia (where Jefferson Davis was later confined).

Belle's image, as it was presented to subsequent generations, by others as well as by herself, was that of a beautiful cloaked courier, racing on horseback up and down the Shenandoah Valley at night for the Confederacy. In fact, she conveyed only one major morsel of information: that of Union Army plans in the Front Royal area.

This aided Stonewall Jackson in a successful attack, inspiring the celebrated cavalry general to express his gratitude in a formal letter.

Since towns of the Shenandoah were constantly changing hands, loyalty to either North or South was precarious. During the Federal occupation of Winchester in August, 1862, Belle was arrested under a warrant signed by the office of Secretary of War Edwin M. Stanton.

She was taken to Washington to begin, with several intermissions, a war-long career as a prisoner. Prison walls proved no deterrent to Belle's romantic inclinations. At the famous "Old Capitol," when not carrying on an affair with a Confederate officer-prisoner, she provided needed entertainment by singing "Maryland, My Maryland!" She also manifested an unfailing insolence toward the guards.

She refused to sign an oath of allegiance, but was released anyhow for lack of charges—only to be arrested again, on suspicion, after she had roamed a few months through the South. The second time she was paroled to recuperate from a prevalent malady, typhoid fever.

Belle's attempt to sail to England aboard the blockade runner *Greyhound* resulted in the capture of the vessel and yet another love affair. Ensign James Hardinge, the Navy's prize master put aboard the *Greyhound*, did see the three-masted steamer into port, but distracted by Belle's seductions, he allowed the Confederate captain to escape. For this inexcusable if nonetheless understandable negligence, Hardinge was court-martialed and discharged from the service.

Belle continued on to London by way of Canada. She made several stage appearances and was received with much acclaim by the English. Their own lusty tastes were reflected in this plain-spoken, rawboned product of West Virginia.

While in the British Isles, she authored, *Belle Boyd in Camp and Prison*, in two fanciful, generally boring volumes. She also married James Hardinge, who thereby proved that neither an ocean nor naval opprobrium could long interrupt the course of true love.

The newlyweds returned to New York, unfortunately before the war was quite over. Back to prison went Belle, who observed Appomattox by gazing disconsolately at the spires of Wilmington through the cell bars of old Fort Delaware. Widowed shortly afterward, Belle married twice again. For two decades she toured the country as a popular lecturer. She died in Wisconsin Dells, Wisconsin, in 1900, of a heart attack, and was buried there.

This was fine with the strait-laced citizenry of her native Martinsburg, where to this day she is considered a village pariah, a very bold and brazen woman indeed. They never wanted even her grave.

There were those of another cut, too, who put down their teacups to indulge in something more dangerous than polite parlor etiquette and parlance—cloak-and-dagger from the drawing room, as it were.

Among this select number was Rose O'Neal Greenhow, the attractive widow of a Washington physician, whose sympathies were torridly Secessionist. In her mid-forties, the patricianlike Mrs. Greenhow swirled about in a social milieu far loftier than that which the country girl Belle Boyd could possibly enjoy. She knew congressmen, statesmen and ranking army and navy officers. With a number of them she was linked romantically. She attended a few White House receptions, although there is no reason to assume that she was acquainted with the President.

Her greatest triumph exploded in the early weeks of the war. She rushed, through her couriers, a cipher message to Richmond that General Irvin McDowell was marching on Manassas, Virginia. This intelligence forewarned the Confederacy and set the stage for the Union debacle of Bull Run, on July 21, 1861.

Overconfident, Mrs. Greenhow stepped up her corre-

spondence with Richmond, detailing the defenses of the
capital and conveying any tidbits of gossip which she happened on. Her nemesis was the pioneer detective, Allen E.
Pinkerton, who placed her under house arrest after inter-
cepting some of her incriminating notes.

Transferred to Old Capitol Prison (where Belle Boyd was
later confined), Rose was surprisingly undeterred. From her
cell she directed a network of at least fifty spies. They included amateur and professional, Southern firebrands, mal-
contents, thrill seekers, representatives of high and low
walks of life.

The Federal government itself was not without traitors.
Accomplices were not hard to come by, even from within a
prison. Some of Rose Greenhow's messages were passed
along in little "presents" she had knitted for her many
friends.

By June, 1862, the War Department resolved to be rid of
"this dangerous and skillful spy." It was quipped embarrass-
ingly of General William B. McClellan, then commanding
the Army of the Potomac, that Mrs. Greenhow invariably
"knew his plans better than Lincoln did." His increasingly
numerous critics would have postscripted that, even so, this
was no feat. The handsome but irresolute general, bogged
down on the Virginia Peninsula, gave no satisfactory explanation to the War Department, with whom he communi-
cated only in demanding more troops.

There was another factor working for Rose Greenhow's
amnesty. Her youngest of four children, Rose, eight, who
had been keeping her mother company in jail, was ailing.

Both mother and daughter were greeted as heroes in
Richmond upon their release. Jefferson Davis already had a
new assignment awaiting "Rebel Rose," as Washington had

come to know her: make friends for the cause in Paris and London.

Mrs. Greenhow was regally entertained first by Napoleon III and next by Queen Victoria. Like Belle Boyd (whom Rose apparently never met), she wrote a book, with the scarcely succinct title: *My Imprisonment and The First Year of Abolition Rule at Washington.* It told nothing of her espionage, not much more of Washington society, was primarily a philippic against the Union spat across more than three hundred venomous but dreary pages.

Rose was virtually engaged to the British Minister to France, Lord Granville, when she embarked for the South in August, 1864. Then, tragedy struck. While being rowed ashore near Wilmington, North Carolina, from the blockade runner *Condor*, Mrs. Greenhow fell overboard and was drowned.

The Rebel cause had lost one of its most able, ardent, and surely most gracious disciples, a woman whose execution even the coldhearted Secretary of War Edwin M. Stanton could not contemplate. By all rules of war and the evidence accumulated against her, he would have had every legal right to seek this punishment from a court-martial. How many boys in blue lay in their graves because of the Rebel Rose?

Less known but as effective in her own limited theater of operations was the hard-boiled hills girl, Nancy Hart. Like Belle Boyd, she provided General Jackson's cavalry with useful intelligence and sometimes led patrols through Union positions in her native West Virginia.

Captured and imprisoned, she grabbed a guard's musket out of his hands, smashed him over the head with the stock, then shot him dead. The muscular and cold-blooded Nancy

escaped to serve the South further as a scout. At the end of
the war she vanished into the limbo of unemployed spies.

The women from Dixie who performed in this branch of
warfare were surely more flamboyant and possibly even
prettier, female for female, than their northerly sisters. But
the Union also could boast its heroines, and effective ones
too—such as Elizabeth van Lew, the inconspicuous spin-
ster.

Miss van Lew, in her early fifties, lived an eminently successful double life in Richmond. She did so without the personal tools used so tellingly by Rose Greenhow and Belle
Boyd. As for Nancy Hart, the mild, sparrowlike Miss van
Lew would no doubt have blanched at the thought of shoul-
dering a rifle, much less discharging it.

Her ordinary appearance had much to do with the ease of
her flitting about Richmond, memorizing defenses here and
there, eavesdropping on any conversations which hinted at
crumbs of military information.

Miss van Lew was commended in several dispatches from
Union generals to the War Department for the "valuable
information" she slipped them. Her other contributions were
unique. In addition to routine intelligence gathering, she
aided Union prisoners to escape from Libby and Belle Isle
prisons, then hid them in her ample mansion on Church Hill,
overlooking the James River.

When he became President, Ulysses Grant thought
enough of her services to Old Glory to award Miss van Lew
the postmistress-ship at Richmond. It paid a munificent
$4,000 a year. Her neighbors in the Virginia capital, how-
ever, never forgave her loyalty to the Old Flag. She was
treated with cold disdain until the day of her death, in 1900,
the same year in which Belle Boyd breathed her last.

More colorful was "Major" Pauline Cushman, a New Orleans-born actress whose heart lay far to the north of Louisiana. In her late twenties at the start of the war, Pauline, of Creole ancestry, was dark, of medium height, described as "handsome" rather than pretty. While she was acting in Nashville in May, 1863, Federal intelligence officers were so impressed with her sense of mimicry that they sought her help in a special plan. They asked her to go to Rebel territory in Shelbyville, fifty miles southeast of Nashville, pretending she was an evicted Southern diehard. Once there she was to obtain all information possible on the plans of General Braxton Bragg, who was believed to be poised to strike.

Pauline gladly went along with the charade, although it nearly cost her life. Captured once, she escaped into the mountains during a blinding rainstorm. She was then caught a second time and sentenced to be hung as a spy. Whether General Bragg would ever have signed her execution papers seemed a matter of conjecture. However, she was freed from the Shelbyville jail by local Union sympathizers as the advancing troops of General William S. Rosecrans drove in to capture the town. Presumably, the Union forces were making use of information Pauline had conveyed to them before her capture.

Pauline's life was never again in jeopardy. However, her knowledge of the highways and backroads of Tennessee, Georgia, Alabama, and Mississippi, gained from one-night stands in dozens of theaters, remained of inestimable value to the Federal armies.

Dressed frequently in a quasi-major's uniform, Pauline played to audiences from Barnum's in New York to Wild West shows in California following the war. Her last years were tragic. Impoverished, she existed through a nightmare of pain from arthritis. She had recently worked as a charwoman when she was found dead in 1893 in a San Francisco boardinghouse. Funds from the Women's Relief Corps of The Grand Army of the Republic and from the response to a newspaper appeal saved "Major" Cushman from the indignity of a pauper's grave in potter's field.

However, her story, though unhappy, was not unique among heroes and heroines. Sometimes, death in battle or before a firing squad was much less cruel than the lingering end in a world which had moved swiftly ahead and forgotten.

There was, for example, the case of Sarah Thompson, whose story is published herewith for the first time since her death. Locked in the vaults of Duke University, in Durham, North Carolina, Sarah's full testimony has recently been exposed to light of day, to permit, as it were, this long-deceased heroine of the Union to speak. In so doing, she leaves, nonetheless, a tantalizing mystery. Was it *really* she who spied and informed on the famous Rebel raider, General John Hunt Morgan?

By the autumn of 1864, when most women spies had already taken their bows, the future of the Confederacy looked dark indeed. Atlanta had fallen, on September 2, to General Sherman's army. Grant was pounding at Petersburg. Sheridan was breathing on the heels of his old opponent, Jubal Early, in the Shenandoah, while the forts guarding Mobile Bay were toppling before Admiral Davy Farragut's invading squadron.

And just north of the sleepy Tennessee hamlet of Greeneville, seventy-five miles east of Knoxville, one of the South's legendary cavalry generals was galloping toward a date with destiny. Morgan, thirty-nine-year-old former Lexington, Kentucky, businessman, had been a persistent deep thorn in the side of his opponents. Whole brigades had been tied down in east Tennessee, Kentucky, Indiana, and southern Ohio just in case this handsome, neatly bearded "thunderbolt," this "great guerilla," or, as his enemies dubbed him, "the great freebooter" should come their way.

His swashbuckling horsemen, who asked only to be known as "Morgan's Men," had caused damage to Union property and military supplies estimated at nearly two million dollars. He had captured at least two thousand Union troops and their officers, paroling most, however, since he moved too fast to be encumbered by prisoners. Morgan's destructive potential was always disproportionate to the strength of his command, which rarely numbered more than two or three thousand.

Daring, resourceful, imaginative, he was a leader who spared neither man nor beast. He rode all day. When his horses could run no farther, he appropriated fresh steeds from any handy source. The war, in the North or South, was hell on farmers and plowing.

Morgan confused his pursuers by tapping telegraph wires and ordering his own operators to transmit false messages to Union telegraphists. He professed his contempt for the enemy in many ways—glaringly so on the night he galloped, with a picked detachment, through the outlying districts of Cincinnati. By the time the Ohioans were aroused to this menace on their very doorsteps, the cavalry raiders were gone. All that attested to their nocturnal visit were little dust spirals in the distance.

In June, 1863, it was one of his patrol groups which had seized Pauline Cushman, who later alluded to the General as "the tenderest of captors." His second marriage, a few months previously, had perhaps served to augment his tenderness.

Three weeks after the Battle of Gettysburg, in July, 1863, the turning of the tide, Morgan was brought to bay near New Lisbon, Ohio. He was hurried off to jail, and the North could at last breathe more easily. His corrosive effect on morale at least equaled his destruction of property.

The state penitentiary at Columbus, however, could not contain this crafty fighter, who was not born to be a jailbird. With six of his companions he tunneled to freedom in April, 1864. These desperate cavalrymen had used table knives as shovels.

Once again, whole Federal units were snatched from their primary tasks of splitting Georgia open and capturing Richmond. Disgustedly, the War Department ordered detachments to ring Morgan's old hunting preserves. The task, however, was no longer so formidable a one. The famed raider was weary, half-sick. His "division" was one in name only. It had shrunken to little more than a band of ragged guerrillas, almost impervious to discipline. By August, Morgan was in trouble.

A board of inquiry had been appointed in Richmond to investigate charges that a group of Morgan's soldiers had, in June, robbed a bank at Mt. Sterling, in eastern Kentucky, and torn jewels off the village women. More damaging yet by the impersonal assessment of warfare, Morgan had been defeated in an engagement at Cynthiana, thirty-five miles northwest of Mt. Sterling.

Under suspicion from his own government, Morgan drew back to his base and home at Abingdon, Tennessee. While tarrying with his beautiful teen-age wife, Martha, he wove desperate plans—plans which might restore the full luster to the old Morgan name. He would, for example, make a daring raid on General Sherman's lines of communications extending south from Chattanooga. Or, and this was of more consequence to General Lee, he would support the hard-pressed Jubal Early in the Shenandoah and along the Maryland border.

But August dragged on with no clear decision as to the most effective employment of Morgan's once-feared command. He grew moody, irresolute, loath to leave Martha's side—except when the great lover experienced the old drives toward other beds. On August 23, these desires just may have sent him seventy miles south from Abingdon to Greeneville, on the Tennessee and Georgia Railroad, near the western slope of the Great Smoky Mountains. (Here Andrew Johnson, the Military Governor of Tennessee, had grown up and was later to be buried after serving as seventeenth President of the United States.) Morgan wanted to stay, as he had previously, at the two-story brick Williams mansion on Irish Street, around the corner from the Episcopal Church and the Fry Hotel.

Dr. Alexander Williams, until his death just prior to the outbreak of war, had been one of Greenville's wealthiest citizens. In addition to his widow, Catharine, he had left a young daughter, Fanny, and three sons. Two of them became officers in the Confederate Army; the third, Joe, remained loyal to Old Glory, though with little luster. He turned into a hard-drinking Union clerk in Knoxville.

Joe's wife Lucy, beautiful and irrepressibly flirtatious, remained in Greeneville, a favorite subject to outrage the town gossips. With her was a younger sister, Jenny Rumbaugh, who, if she were of Lucy's emotional coloring, was more discreet.

Since one of the Williams' sons was on General Morgan's

staff, there was at least a possibility that the officer rather than the sexy Lucy had drawn the cavalry leader to Greeneville. However, Morgan's past record with women might be admissible evidence to the contrary. The fact that the General on a previous visit had discovered a wounded Union officer in the Williams home did not deter him from subsequent sojourns.

On August 21, Morgan galloped out of Greeneville again. The Richmond newspapers reported that he had left with the "intent" of marching on Knoxville. In view of Morgan's poorly armed troops, the supposition was absurd.

Frustrated, Morgan still wanted to do something, something which might also remove the blot of Mt. Sterling. Finally it occurred to him that the inconsiderable Union cavalry detachment at Bull's Gap, sixteen miles northwest of Greeneville, would be easy pickings. And, en route, he could tarry another night at the Williamses'.

A hard-riding but little known horseman, Major General Alvan C. Gillem, was in command of the cavalry brigades at Bull's Gap. A solemn, businesslike officer, he had every reason to complain that he had already spent too much of the war chasing after John Hunt Morgan in these southeastern states.

On a drizzling Saturday, September 3, Morgan arrived with approximately sixteen hundred of his men in Greeneville. He could muster no greater force. The inhabitants watched once more as the horses kicked up the mud and red clay. The mixed Unionists and Secessionists of this border-country town were already accustomed to Confederate cavalry. Only in March a portion of General Nathan Bedford Forrest's troops had bivouacked there.

Morgan was undeniably careless in returning to a house where a daughter-in-law was married to a Union clerk, and where an enemy officer had been secreted. On the other hand, Lucy Williams could neither hurt nor comfort John Morgan on this visit. She happened to be staying overnight at College Farm, owned by her mother-in-law, located four miles from Greeneville.

The cavalry leader, however, could have had reason to fear someone else, someone who had been biding her time since January 10, waiting for revenge. On that day, Sarah Thompson, twenty-five-year-old mother of two little girls, had been widowed.

Sylvanis Thompson and Sarah Thompson were strong Unionists. Their sympathies could be dangerous in east Tennessee, where houses of residents so minded were sometimes broken into and pilfered, the men tarred and feathered or beaten until senseless. Sarah herself had witnessed a merciless flogging of a man who was strapped to a log and given thirty-nine lashes.

The couple did what they could to frustrate the Confederacy. After joining the First Tennessee Cavalry, USA, as a private, Sylvanis was appointed to recruiting, a hazardous service in Tennessee. Even so, his wife aided his work.

"I would," she recalled, "get the men up and take them to him by night and he would take them through the lines to the Union forces."

In this way, by her estimates, she had moved out five hundred recruits, always at the greatest personal hazard. The forested area was a hive of Confederate irregulars and bushwhackers, who were the scum of the South, no better than brigands and murderers. Seized several times and grazed by a bullet once, Sarah always succeeded in talking her way to freedom.

Her husband was not so lucky. Captured while carrying a message to General Ambrose Burnside, commanding in

Knoxville, he was jailed at Belle Isle Prison, on the James River. He escaped and a reward was offered for his capture.

In January, just resuming his recruiting service, Sylvanis was shot and killed near Greeneville—murdered either by irregulars or bushwhackers attached to Morgan's former command after his recapture or by snipers from ambush. The manner of his death was never certain.

Sarah redoubled her own work against the Confederacy, swearing somehow to make it pay for her husband's death.

In July she completed a 110-mile round trip to Knoxville on horseback. Her saddlebags were filled with Union dispatches and recruiting information. And still, so late in the conflict, she operated at peril of her life, as she wrote, "it was not safe to express your sentiment. You could see Rebels around your house at all times, watching, by day and night."

It was about 3:00 P.M. when Sarah became aware of a "rush in the streets." She turned from her stove where she was "preparing something for Sunday—tomato butter." It was a treat which her children, Lilly and Harriet, contemplated with the greatest impatience all week long. She put down her stirring ladle and walked to the door. Then, she reported, "I was surprised to see John Morgan, the Rebel raider, who was feared by all who knew him and a great many who did not know him—for he was the fiend of the South."

Although on his last visit Morgan had continued around the corner to Irish Street and the Williamses' handsome residence, this time Sarah Thompson was surprised all the more when the cavalry general pulled up his horse sharply in front of her own house and dismounted. He strolled to her porch, then paused, filled his pipe, and started smoking it.

In a confiding mood, not wholly uncommon in the presence of the opposite sex, Morgan declared he was going to Knoxville, and when he arrived there he would send for her. She would, Sarah recalled his asserting, "make some Rebel a good wife," but he postscripted, if she were "as good a Rebel as a damn Union woman."

He "used a great deal of flattery," though for what purpose she did not conjecture when she wrote down the sequence of events of that wet weekend. This "flattery," however, served to make her "mad." Her disposition was in no degree improved when several of Morgan's cavalrymen shouldered their way into the house, removed all the tomato butter from its caldron, and heaped it onto dishes. They left, with butter, dishes, also loaves of bread, and even Sarah's breadbasket.

When she implored Morgan to protect her, he "laughed me to scorn." He told her not to fear "for I have never starved and they had to live and the Union women had to help feed them."

With that, the General relit his pipe and splashed from the shelter of the porch back out into the rain. He continued on to the Williams house.

Sarah noticed that he had posted pickets throughout Greeneville and around the mansion, which she thought of as a place of "grandeur, one of the wealthy homes in this hill town." Like the other women of Greeneville, Sarah envied the status and apparent good life the elegant abode represented.

However, this particular wet night the widow of Sylvanis Thompson was thankful that there was a Williams mansion in which General Morgan could absent himself.

Sarah was experienced in a battle of wits against the Confederates, even if she had not won every encounter. She had learned by cold experience to make the best of opportunities when offered, and not to wait for a second chance.

She knew, through east Tennessee's silent citizenry of Unionists, that there was an effective if not large force of Federal cavalry at Bull's Gap. She could assume that Morgan was considering a move against this enemy—*when* he was ready. Tonight, however, he was "fixin' for a good time." By morning he would, for some hours, be too weary, drugged, and hung over to mount an attack.

If Sarah were to avenge her husband this was her invitation. She must act and act fast.

She glanced at the empty stove, empty pans, and looted bread cupboard, then toward her two hungry children. She put on a bonnet, worn riding boots and a heavy cloak against the rain, then picked up a tin pail.

Sarah started for the door, but paused. She thought of the colored woman, Flora, who helped around the house and watched over the children. She preferred not to think of her as a slave, nor did she treat her as one. She walked to the small house in the rear yard where the woman lived.

"Flora, I'm going away overnight," Sarah explained. "You keep an eye on the Williams house. If General Morgan leaves, you tell me. Understand, Flora?"

Pail in hand, she walked to the edge of town. A sentry, placed there by Morgan, challenged her.

"My cows are in that pasture, over there," she explained, gesturing. "It is time to milk them."

Half-incredulous, the picket scratched his head, then motioned her on.

Sarah sloshed through the muddy lane at a normal gait in order not to arouse suspicion. Not until she attained and crossed over the brow of the first hill did she break into a run. She had not lied altogether. Several of the cows in the wide community pasture were hers. But she had no time this late, wet afternoon to milk them.

Instead, tossing her pail aside, she raced as fast as she could through a cornfield to the house of a friend "who had aided me more than one time." There she borrowed a horse.

For a city girl, unused to the empty countryside and forests at night and also, quite likely, unused to horseback riding, Sarah's journey into the storm and blackness would have seemed horrifying, if not implausible. However, Sarah had been daring darkness and the enemy the war long.

Keeping close to the railroad tracks, she led her horse over Chuckey Creek, now swollen from the downpour. Pausing only to give the animal brief rests and to listen for sounds of Confederate patrols, Sarah rode on beside the railroad. There were no trains on this section.

Farther to the east, where it wound into Virginia, the line was controlled by the South. West of Bull's Gap, serving the Federal cause, it became a mainline for the armies in blue which were holding Tennessee.

As the evening wore on, without hint of the storm's abating, Sarah galloped past the slumbering darkened communities of Gustaves, Midway, Mosheim, Myers, and finally she was fording Lick Creek. Bull's Gap was near.

As she expected, it was not many more minutes before the yellow flicker of a bobbing light grew larger. Soon, through the slanting rain a throaty challenge: "Halt!"

Sarah obeyed. She shouted: "Friend! A Union woman!"

Now she could see the grizzled face of a mounted sentry, holding aloft his kerosene lantern. His rifle, with great trust, was in the saddle holster.

"I have important information for General Gillem," she persisted.

The patrol wearily wiped the rain from his face, then beckoned her to follow him. In a few minutes she was in a small frame house requistioned by General Gillem.

The commanding officer was sleepy this midnight hour. He seemed to Sarah to be scornful of her report, convinced as he was that Morgan was still at Abingdon.

"A woman's tale," he sniffed.

However, she won over two champions on Gillem's staff: Colonel John S. Brownlow of the Third Tennessee Cavalry and Lieutenant Edward J. Brooks of the Tenth Michigan. Brownlow "talked up" the proposal of surprising General Morgan on its military merits, while Brooks vouched for Sarah's past performance.*

General Gillem agreed to send a probing force into Greeneville. Sarah recalled, "at last they started though I must say Gillem did not deserve any of the honor. If left to him, he would not have went!"

Before they started, Sarah had one request—hairpins. Miraculously, the Union officers were able to supply her want.

Approximately a hundred cavalrymen, picked from the Tenth Michigan, together with the Third, Ninth, Twelfth, and Thirteenth Tennessee regiments, clattered off into the night. Sarah, on a fresh mount, rode with them.

Morgan, meanwhile, as dawn arrived, still slept. Presumably, he had enjoyed the "good time" Sarah had envisioned.

---

* Later he wrote an affidavit: "She was very often engaged as a spy. She had been a shorter time before up as far as Wytheville, Virginia, on a spying expedition for us and brought her information to us at Strawberry Plains, Tennessee, and returned to Greeneville, having been very seriously injured by the fall of her horse when Rebels were in pursuit of her."

Certainly the girls, Fanny Williams and Jenny Rumbaugh, were home, and the cavalry general loved teen-agers, even as other men might savor rare wine or gourmet cooking.

Shortly before seven o'clock, one of his staff officers, himself chilled, sent out for brandy, if any could be confiscated in Greeneville. He would get it to his sentries who were drenched through. They must be warmed and fed if they were to mount a surprise attack later in the day upon Bull's Gap.

The men, however, never tasted the brandy. A sentry on the far perimeter of Greeneville shouted: "The Yankees . . .!"

The alarm echoed, too late, to the Williams house. General Morgan was shaken awake. He stumbled out of bed, drawing on only a pair of pants over his nightclothes.

"Where are they?" he asked his hostess as he clomped downstairs, obviously aware belatedly that he had committed a commanding officer's fatal mistake—that of underestimating his foe.

"Everywhere," Mrs. Williams replied.

With an aide, he ran out through the back door, across the grounds of the estate to Main Street, where he ducked momentarily into the small rickety Fry Hotel. That did not seem sufficient sanctuary, so he dashed out again and into the cellar of the adjoining Episcopal Church.

The Union troops now were galloping through the morning drizzle into Greeneville like precursors of doom. Morgan's pickets melted before their musket and pistol fire. Some of the horsemen had merely to brandish their sabers.

But, *where* was the main body of Morgan's command? It had numbered sixteen hundred only the past afternoon.

Sarah rode to her home, where the children were asleep. Her mission had been accomplished—almost.

It was apparent that the target of her exertions had fled. Sarah asked Flora if she had been keeping an eye on the Williams house as instructed, and if so, did she know where General Morgan was now?

The servant indicated, with a sweep of her hand, that Morgan was still somewhere on these premises. Sarah was sufficiently convinced so that she drew on dry wraps and left her house, walking toward Depot Street, bordering the Williams estate on the south.

The Southern general had concluded in these final ticking minutes that the church offered no better refuge than the Fry Hotel. He ran out and back through the trees and shrubbery of the Williamses' lawns, finally sliding under the white board fence surrounding the grape arbor. Its entwining natural labyrinth seemed a secure place of concealment.

The "great guerilla," however, had made a final miscalculation, even as he had in discounting the possibilities of betrayal and surprise.

Events now accelerated to such a pace that none could be quite positive of their exact sequence or even character. Sarah, arriving by chance outside the fenced arbor, was certain she spotted the pajama-and trousers-clad silhouette of Morgan below the vines. As she was to reconstruct the scene, she then hailed the first Union cavalrymen to pass by, advising him: "Sir, if you will tear the fence down I assure you you will find Morgan!"

This soldier, Private Andrew Campbell, of Company G, the Thirteenth Regiment, Tennessee Volunteer Cavalry,*

---

* Campbell, rewarded with a lieutenancy for his work, did not mention, subsequently, that anyone led him to the arbor. His impression was that he had first noticed Morgan hiding.

started to pull a board away, recognized General Morgan, and called on him to give himself up.

"I'll never surrender!" Private Campbell was to quote Morgan in reply. It sounded in character, since the cavalry leader had several times boasted he would never be taken alive.

Campbell, observing Morgan starting to reach for what could have been a pistol, raised his rifle, took point-blank aim and fired.

The heavy slug, bigger than a modern 45-caliber bullet, hit Morgan, as Sarah noted, "near the middle." The impact knocked him back and rolled him over, deeper inside the vines.

"Oh God!" he gasped audibly. These were his last words.

Campbell tore off another of the whitewashed boards, then dove, like a rabbit hound, in after his quarry.

Morgan was dead. Only a dark red stain on his under-garments, in the center of his chest, spreading toward his abdomen, lent color to the ashen-white skin of the long-feared raider, who, in unbelievable seconds, had become just another corspe.

At this point, one of the General's staff officers, identified as a Lieutenant "X" Hawkins, arrived in time only to be captured—as, ultimately, were all of Morgan's lieutenants.

The body was placed on a horse—not dragged *by* a horse, as some Confederate sources alleged—and carried just outside the town. By nightfall, the dead commander's brother-in-law and senior staff officer, Colonel Basil Duke, was paroled to take the remains back to Abingdon.

However, a flurry of shooting developed between the remaining Morgan forces and Gillem's fresh, whooping horsemen, streaming into Greeneville. They were electrified by the news they had so long waited to hear.

"Morgan is dead!"

One Confederate dashed into Sarah's house, where she herself had taken refuge from the "cannonballs" which she observed "fell thick and fast."

The furious Rebel threatened—"The rope was there to hang me"—but Sarah did not lose heart, since "God has so often cared for me and I knew he would not let me down this time."

For minutes which seemed an eternity, her captor "swore and raged, while the bullets fell like hail." Then, suddenly the "blue clads" of the Tenth Michigan burst to her rescue, capturing the enemy soldier as they did so.

It was all over. The great Morgan was dead. His "guerrillas" had been routed, seventy-five killed and one hundred prisoners, including the slain general's staff, taken. Field-pieces and innumerable muskets also become Union trophies.

The next day, Gillem dispatched to Knoxville headquarters: "I surprised, defeated and killed John Morgan at Greeneville this morning . . . the enemy's force outnumbered mine but the surprise was complete."

Two days later, the Richmond papers, in announcing the death, attributed the loss to the work of "the wife of one villanous officer on Burnside's staff."

Sarah Thompson could not be allowed to remain in Greeneville. General Gillem loaded her, her two girls and Flora into an ambulance Monday afternoon, September 5, and took her to Knoxville. There (and subsequently in Cleveland) she served out the war months as a matron in Federal hospitals.

The Confederacy, in offering a reward for her capture,

thus affirmed whom they believed responsible for the death of the Rebel raider.

Lucy Williams, too, was removed beyond the wrath of Confederate townspeople. Her husband Joe arrived post-haste and carried her, too, to Knoxville, where obviously he should have long before kept her under his scrutiny.*

Gillem did not clarify the sources of Morgan's betrayal. In later reports he alluded vaguely to "men" informers. Samuel Scott, the historian of the Thirteenth Tennessee, who nonetheless was not present at Morgan's death or during the chain of circumstances leading ot it, wrote of a twelve-or thirteen-year-old boy, one James Leady, "said" to have borne the tidings to Bull's Gap that rainy September night.

Sarah was fortunate, however, in obtaining general endorsement from her old neighbor, Andrew Johnson, who certified her to be of "the highest respectability and unquestionably loyal." This testimonial he signed in Nashville in November, 1864. It was among the last acts as Military Governor of Vice President-elect Andrew Johnson. Inauguration was but weeks away, and April and Ford's Theater, a few fateful weeks more.

After the war, Sarah made a short lecture tour. Some believed her experiences as she recounted them, others did not. All seemed to enjoy listening to this pert, plucky daughter of the Tennessee hills.

On January 1, 1866, she married an army veteran, Orville Bacon, of Broome County, New York. She bore two more children, one of whom she described as a "cripple," who died when he was thirteen.

Mrs. Bacon moved to Washington in 1877, when she was

---

* Lucy, in September, 1865, filed for divorce. Her husband, in his rejoinder, at least absolved his wife from complicity in Morgan's killing, noting, "and he [Joe Williams] has been informed that the information was given by another and different woman altogether."

widowed for the second time. She was in dire need of employment, and fortunately she obtained a $600-a-year clerical position with the Treasury Department.

Her job lasted but a year when she was summarily discharged "by reason of the exhaustion of the fund from which you have been paid."

Impoverished, ailing, with children to care for, Sarah Thompson Bacon wrote pitiful letters to Congress and to the War Department. She was bitter not only from her own experience but from the example of too many in the nation's capital idling through plush, relatively well-paid jobs. Her hurt and despair found voice in a meandering poem which she circulated in Congress' halls. One stanza read:

> One hour of throbbing war outweighs
>   With all its mad sublimity
> A cycle of these plotting days
>   Where cunning crowds out chivalry
> When like a begger she must wait
>   With Honor's scars from morn 'till eve'
> That shoddy at his golden gate
>   May patronize the empty sleeve.

Sarah obtained letters from former officers stationed at Bull's Gap, who reaffirmed her role in the death of Morgan. Among them were Colonel Brownlow, Lieutenant Brooks and Lieutenant John G. Johnson, of the Thirteenth Tennessee Cavalry. Brownlow, however, subsequently confused the record by attributing the information to a male informer.

The impact of their testimony was to reinstate Sarah in Federal service, this time as an investigator in the Postal Inspector's office. She enjoyed the work, which she found reminiscent of her war adventures.

Later in the 1880's she married her third husband, James W. Cotten. Once more, she was prematurely widowed. By the 1890's, however, the aging, shriveling Sarah Cotten had at least established her claim to a war widow's benefits, even though meager, and to a pension for her nursing service. The latter, amounting to twelve dollars a month, required a special act of the Fifty-fifth Congress, in 1899.

The Bill (S.1837) had the effect of lending congressional endorsement to her role in the death of Morgan. Noting that her "service in the cause of the Union, aside from her services as a nurse," were "*correctly*" set forth in the Senate report preceding the bill, the measure reiterated the testimony of Lieutenant Brooks, of the Tenth Michigan, and also of Major General S. G. Carter, Provost Marshal General of east Tennessee.

Carter, affirming her previous intelligence work, added, "I believe without thought of recompense or reward . . . Sarah Thompson gave the intelligence of General Morgan . . . which led to the defeat and death of that noted rebel."

In her limited circle in Washington, Sarah became a familiar figure. She rarely missed a lodge night of the Women's Relief Corps, GAR. She was a faithful communicant of the Hamline Methodist Church, where she was known as "Mother Thompson."

When she retired from the Post Office in 1903, Sarah went to live with her son, Orville Bacon, Jr., on Capital Hill. She frequently visited her daughter, Mrs. Harriet Lipp, in suburban Hyattsville.

Her health failed; her dark hair turned snow white. She managed nonetheless to keep up small daily errands and attend church services on Sunday. Then, one April morning, 1909, Sarah left her son's home for the post office, a customary morning errand and an excuse to chat with old friends.

Waiting for the electric streetcar to take her back, she somehow was caught between two trolleys and knocked down. Although her skull was severely fractured and she remained unconscious, Sarah lived for two days.

She died in her seventy-first year, a plucky, wiry daughter of Tennessee who accomplished what many regiments of Federal infantry and cavalry had been unable to do for three frustrating years—the elimination of one of the North's most implacable foes.

Sarah was buried in Arlington Cemetery with full military honors. A granddaughter, Mrs. Ora Lipp Morris, one of the number of descendants still living in the Washington area, recalls to this day the rifle volleys echoing across the slopes of the final resting place for the nation's heroes. Sarah's grave was among the first in a section which would fill with her sister nurses of wars to come.

Her small, regulation headstone is today all but lost in a sea of weathering markers from a nearly forgotten war, remembered only on Memorial Day when other old ladies faithfully bedeck the hallowed ground with little bright flags.

3

⁞

THE "ALICE SERVICE"

•⇢ Louise de Bettignies, 1915

Sarah Thompson's cup had overflowed with misfortune and unhappiness. Had fate, then, been altogether cruel in projecting her into the path of an oncoming trolley? If the aged, infirm Sarah had lived just five years more, she would have witnessed, if from afar, history's worst war.

Kaiser Wilhelm's military machine was in high gear when it pounded into Belgium that flaming August, 1914. No one had foreseen its crushing force. Brussels fell in three weeks. Two days later, goose-stepping soldiers were at the gates of the industrial center Lille.

The mayor of this historically disputed French city, in the center of rich coal fields near the River Lys and astride the road to Dunkirk, did not wish to preside over a wasteland of rubble. He declared Lille "open"!

General Alexander von Kluck, commanding the powerful First Army, paused in his Channel dash. Patrols ordered into Lille's suburbs found no street barricades or strong points. The Citadel appeared to have been evacuated.

The Germans swept on. On August 30, Amiens echoed to the measured cadence of tens of thousands of army boots, and was submerged under a serried sea of spiked helmets. On September 4, Rheims was occupied.

Then, before the Marne and within a few miles of Paris, the invader was stopped. Von Schlieffen's plan had failed. The armies, having outraced their supplies, had to contend not only with the French but with a British Expeditionary Force now clawing out like cornered tigers.

Back, back, rolled the long waves of field gray. The French reoccupied Rheims and Amiens. The Germans, in anger, trained their siege guns on Rheims' beautiful cathedral. From Paris flashed the order to hold stubbornly onto all ground still out of enemy hands.

The garrison returned to Lille.

The British, at a price, recaptured Ypres. Now the enemy vented his fury on Lille, south of Ypres, fearful that the main battle lines on the western front would be outflanked. After a heavy bombardment, Lille capitulated on October 12.

Caught up in this maelstrom was a group of professional and semiprofessional doctors and nurses, as well as untrained recruits who were mostly Red Cross volunteers. The military medical staffs alone were unable to care for the ever welling flood of wounded. Long lines of ambulances rolled to and from the front lines. Private houses were commandeered as hospitals and dressing stations.

Among these many ladies and young girls in white uniforms with the familiar, evocative red insignia was Louise Marie Jeanne Henriette de Bettignies, the pretty, darkhaired daughter of a Lille porcelain manufacturer of the past century, Henri de Bettignies, and his wife, the former

Mabille de Poncheville. The seventh of eight children, the petite yet sturdy Louise came of noble lineage tracing back to the courts of the first Louis.

Her upbringing was quiet, refined, undistinguished from that of thousands of other French girls born into upper bourgeois families. She could have grown into adulthood and retraced the patterns of, for example, her mother had not a war intervened and turned the courses of human lives while at the same time altering the destinies and the boundaries of nations.

When Henri de Bettignies died, Louise made a surprising and as well epochal decision for one of her society and background. She decided to attend Oxford. She became one of the first women to go to class at the famous English university, although she was still some three decades too early to be eligible for a degree. There the young lady from Lille studied mostly English, Latin, and literature. She already spoke Flemish in addition to her native tongue.

Louise returned to Lille to continue studies at that city's own university. An unusually well educated and poised young lady, she spent the next decade as a governess with the nobility in Italy and Austria. She refused, for reasons unclear, to care for the children of Archduke Franz Ferdinand, heir apparent to the Austro-Hungarian throne, whose assassination at Sarajevo, on June 28, 1914, precipitated the Great War.

She combined all the qualities parents could desire in the protector and teacher of their children. She was intelligent, educated, charming, and also athletic. She excelled in golf, swimming, and running. She was fleet as a doe, a physical prowess which would be especially useful in the nearing years.

Yet, strangely, Louise de Bettignies commenced to shrink from her outgoing life. She returned home with every intention of taking the vows of a nun. Perhaps she was inspired by the example of her brother, Henri, Jr., a priest at Orsinval, to the south; perhaps by an unhappy love affair while a governess in Italy or Austria. She kept no diary. Those who were favored by her correspondence treasured it to themselves.

The fathers at St. Joseph College, Lille, advised Louise to wait, think it over. Not yet thirty-five, this woman with a sparkle in her eyes and an obvious love of life did not appear ready for the cloisters. She agreed. As a compromise, she became a Red Cross nurse. When the war broke out, she was working at the Daughters of Charity clinic on the Boulevard Vauban. As soon as the enemy forces arrived in Lille, they occupied every available hospital bed.

In the first days, a German surgeon asked, "Does anyone here understand my language?"

The other girls continued with their duties, paying him no attention, whether or not they could speak some German. Louise, however, admitted she did.

A badly wounded young Bavarian soldier wished to dictate a letter to his mother.

"I am," he spoke, "about to die. Before I do, mother, I wish to say that war is horrible. There is nothing good about it. It is all wrong. . . ."

He continued without restraint. Louise wrote as he dictated. Then she addressed the envelope for him and left it and the letter by his side. By morning, as he himself had foreseen, the soldier was dead.

Louise had evidence all around her in substantiation of the Bavarian's dying sentiments, evidence far more provocative than the sight of machine-gun nests at every street intersection. Lille was a shambles. In ruins were the Grand and Continental Hotels, the once magnificent Café Jean, the Grande Pharmacie de France, as well as all of the Rue Faidherbe and the Rue du Vieux-Marche-aux-Poulets. Partially destroyed were the Rue de Bethune, the Rue de L'Hopital Militaire, and the Rue du Molinel.

Henri de Bettignies' seventh-born acted in character with her impetuous nature. She decided to take a far more active part in the war. Discarding her Red Cross uniform and cloaks, she donned the plain clothes of a middle-class village woman and started south. Her purposes were mixed: to gather scraps, any available scraps, of military information as well as to determine how many villagers in this section of France were prepared to help her frustrate the German invader.

She went first to Peronne, forty-five miles south of Lille, then northeast to Cambrai and Solesmes. She memorized all that she thought could conceivably be of help to the French or British armies. Louise was impressed, for example, by columns of German troops detraining at Solesmes, with "red and white cap badges, red collars with the numeral 110."

Then, at Orsinval, she paused at the church of her brother. Torn between the neutrality historically expected of men of the cloth and patriotism, Father de Bettignies indicated he would aid her in "passive . . . quiet ways."

Louise returned to Lille long enough to join two other young women and a male guide. They crossed the border between Courtrai and Harelbeke, Holland. From there the four boarded a train for Ostend, where ferries still tossed across the Channel several times daily in defiance of patrolling U-boats and German destroyers. In fact, Admiral von

Scheer's glowering High Seas Fleet was less than a day's steaming to the east, in Wilhelmshaven roadstead, just behind the shadowy Borkum reefs.

The cross-Channel ferry to Folkestone was crowded with refugees, businessmen, social figures, military officials, and—unquestionably—spies. For those travelers still attempting to return home after being caught up in war's sudden vortex, the experience was unforgettable.

Every seat was filled with sleepers. The few available cabins were relinquished to women and children. Single men gallantly helped mothers overburdened with young ones and even lent them money when necessary. Among the bedspread bundles and straw suitcases occasional oversized hatboxes, bearing gay Paris labels or, perhaps, men's familiar pigskin valises "made in Germany" struck a discordant note.

To Louise, this was coming home.

British customs, security police, and an infiltrating assortment of counterintelligence agents from Scotland Yard, the Ministry of War, and other governmental departments endeavored to sort out the motley throngs pouring down the gangplanks. The most decrepit or innocent-appearing old peasant woman could as well be the most dangerous.

Her lumpy pack could contain anything from radio transmitters to heavy Lugers. Inside the hem of her dress' wrinkled folds could be printed, perhaps in invisible ink, a volume of instructions for the other agents known to be operating throughout the British Isles in these early weeks of the war.

Louise de Bettignies evoked official scrutiny by announcing she wished to return to France, this time to St. Omer, west of Lille and a headquarters for the BEF.

"*Why*," she was asked, "do you choose St. Omer?"

She replied she thought she could be useful there.

Louise then told of her meanderings south of Lille, casually ticking off what she had observed of the German troops. When she told of the "red and white cap badges, red collars with the numeral 110" on the soldiers clomping onto the sidings at Solesmes, the major's eyes brightened.

"The 110th Bavarian Cavalry!" he exclaimed. "They were in action at Cambrai—ruddy tough fellows, too!"

Impressed with her report of what were obviously reinforcements moving the few miles west from Solesmes, the major wrote her a pass to his superiors in London. There, they listened to the story of the bright-eyed refugee from Lille, and believed her.

She would, just as she desired, be returned to France, behind the lines to organize the gathering of information about the enemy and his plans and then endeavor to transmit it to the Allies. It was also hoped she could aid in the spiriting through enemy lines of escaped prisoners of war or Belgians and Frenchmen of military age. Any counterintelligence she could effect would be just that much of a bonus.

There was, in spite of fanciful reports to the contrary, no spy school as such in England, nothing, for example, to compare with a made-in-Germany version established by a nebulous woman known as "Fraulein Doktor" at 10 Rue d'Etang de Schoonbeke, Antwerp.

Through intensive talks and "briefings" with experienced intelligence officers she was advised of the rudiments of this clandestine profession: about secret inks, codes, and unusual hiding places for messages. True names would never be used. Louise herself now became "Alice Dubois." Her immediate contact in Holland was known as a "letter box," and

would variously be identified only as "Mr. Beemans," or
sometimes "Aunt Emma." Conceivably, "Mr. Beemans,"
could be a fisherman and "Aunt Emma" a village prostitute,
or even vice versa.

The English did not prolong her informal schooling. The
war was urgent. On a blustery February morning "Alice
Dubois," supplied with papers attesting that she was a
representative of a Dutch "cereal company," walked off the
Channel steamer onto the busy wharves of Flushing. Unquestionably, she was not the only disguised agent to debark
or to study the faces of those who were arriving.

Louise was not challenged until she crossed the border at
Bouschaute, where a village policeman kept insisting that
she must be a German spy.

"*What* cereal company?" he kept asking.

She finally was allowed to pass.

Louise continued on to Orsinval, once more visiting her
priest-brother. Then she returned northward to Lille. The
city was silent, under a light mantle of snow which cloaked
the ruins with a frozen grandeur. The only traffic was that of
the German military. Even the reassuring grind over cobblestones of the iron-rimmed wheels of carts carrying pro-
visions, milk, or wine and the bark of the dogs which drew
them were heard but infrequently.

Then she was hurrying past the shuttered windows of her
own street, the Rue d'Isly. She paused at a familiar door,
pulled the bell cord. The door was opened cautiously, characteristic lately of the oppressed inhabitants of Lille. A well-
known face poked through the opening, stared, then broke
into smiles.

"Mon Dieu!" squealed the elderly maid of the De Bettignies. "C'est mademoiselle!"

From then on Louise's career was as spectacular as it was brief. For one whose life had been largely sheltered and ordered in concert with others, she showed surprising organizational ability. Her first move was to appoint an assistant, a shopkeeper some ten years her junior from the nearby community of Roubaix, close to the Belgian border: Marie Leonie van Houtte, a tough-willed patriot who had already aided several young men to escape to Holland. Her code name became "Charlotte."

The "Alice Service," as Louise's network came to be known, grew quickly and with spontaneity. Because of her knowledge of the country and friends from childhood, she enlisted helpers in communities as far south in the Artois province as Cambrai and Bapaume, north in Picardy to the Channel coast at Dunkirk, and east through occupied Belgium into the heart of Brussels.

Unquestionably, Louise had no idea of exactly how many were engaged in her "service," any more than the agents and couriers themselves were aware of the identities of the many "letter boxes" who collected their bits of information.

That the operation was effective and posed a threat to the conqueror was attested by the increasing numbers of counteragents and informers rushed to the Lille region by Colonel Walther Nicolai, chief of the German Army's *Nachrichten Abteilung,* or intelligence department, sometimes known as the father of modern secret service. Captain Hermann Himmel, a reserve officer nominally attached to General von Gebsottel's 111th Bavarian Cavalry, working indirectly for Nicolai in Lille, became Louise's immediate nemesis.

From the outset, "Alice Dubois" was under surveillance. In her various disguises as a seller of lace or cheese, a peasant girl, or a schoolteacher, she was shadowed by Himmel's men. In railroad stations, in shops, and on street corners, during her almost incessant wanderings, she was accosted by successive strangers who attempted with innocent-sounding questions to induce her to betray herself.

"Pardon me, mademoiselle," a "fish peddler" might ask. "Do you happen to know the address of Madame Croissant?"

If Madame Croissant was a link in the "Alice Service," as she presumably was, Louise would shake her head, shrug, and walk on. As she grew emboldened by her own success, Louise did not hesitate to snap back: "Mind your own business!" or even to provoke outbursts which enlisted the support of casual passersby.

Once, when an overbearing Oberst berated a shopkeeper, within Louise's hearing, for not speaking the German language, she herself replied in the officer's tongue with such a sharp torrent of abuse that he was left speechless and blinking. The organizer of the "Alice Service" fled into the anonymity of the sidewalk traffic.

She had learned early the effectiveness of suddenly swinging, when cornered, onto the offensive. It was a disarming and arrogant technique that blended in complete harmony with the character of Himmel's own bullies. These included women as well as men. His female police were known as the "Green Devils," from the color of their uniforms. One, especially annoying to the Alice Service, was dubbed the "Frog," because of her singular resemblance to that squat amphibian.

Always these policewomen were demanding to see the *cartes d'identité* of the French citizens—passes issued by the occupation forces bearing description and photograph. They were not foolproof, as Himmel soon discovered.

Two Lille residents, Georges de Geyter and Joseph Willot,

adapted their skill as civil engineers first to photography, next to printing. They could duplicate an identification card so faithfully in all details that no laboratory short of the *Nachrichtendienst's* in Berlin could prove it a forgery.

This inventive pair went a step further. They impregnated with a powerful camera lens almost invisible messages onto celluloidlike negatives, which could be read only when projected onto a screen. These thin transparencies were then placed over the identity cards—until the enemy, suspicious, decreed that the passes could no longer be covered.

From De Geyter's home at 132 Rue de la Station also came the resistance newspaper, *l'Oiseau de France*, a junior version of the famed *La Libre Belgique*, of Brussels. To be seen reading it was a serious offense. For distributing it Belgians had already been shot. The clever printers, however, always managed to move out their presses a jump ahead of the raiding parties.

Elise de Geyter, the wife of *l'Oiseau*'s publisher, was arrested several times on suspicion of circulating the contraband journal of Lille. Her glib tongue always saved her. Never brought to trial, she invariably walked out of Himmel's headquarters within hours of her seizure.

This constant game of tag, in which the nimble Elise was always "it," underscored the paradoxical sense of legality dominating the German mind in the Great War. Without a whimper or the flicker of an eyelash, the enemy would only too gladly have blindfolded her before one of the already well-used stakes in the Citadel, now a German barracks and rifle range.

But the secret police weren't satisfied. They just did not possess the exact evidence they wanted to execute her. It did not have to be much, nor in saner times or by other moral or judicial standards especially grave—just a line or two, and then the rifles could bark, and the official report, in quintuplicate, could go back to Berlin, nicely in order, all paragraphs completed and formal questions answered, a thoroughly satisfactory "legal" execution.

In spite of all countermeasures and hazards, Louise's couriers were within a very few months rivaling the French postal service in the volume of messages slipped across the Dutch border, to other agents in occupied Brussels, or west to Allied headquarters. Methods, while not invariable original, nonetheless required painstaking preparation.

Messages were engraved sometimes inside a rosary or coded in invisible ink upon the butterfly headgear of the Sisters of Charity. For a while, they were placed, handily enough, beneath the gummed labels of matchboxes. This expedient had to be abandoned altogether when too many security policemen simply requisitioned the matches to keep their always soggy pipe tobacco smoldering.

Chocolate bar wrappers also were found impractical as correspondence paper for the same reason. Much of what was edible or drinkable was confiscated by the ever ravenous border guards.

Cigarettes presented great possibilities. The rice paper wrapper itself could be inscribed with invisible ink, or a more substantial communication could replace most of the tobacco. However, not only were enemy agents and minor police functionaries constantly "requisitioning" smokes from the populace, but they eventually became suspicious whenever a suspect lit one of his own cigarettes or cigars. Indeed he probably was destroying evidence (an emergency device which saved lives again in the second World War).

More than once, important communications—blueprints,

for example, of enemy fortifications or stolen operational plans of conceivably an entire battalion or even regiment— were slipped into neutral territory in a ghoulish but effective fashion: within a coffin. To make detection seemingly impossible, the papers were wrapped tightly in a small glass tube and inserted surgically into the corpse's windpipe. Obviously, there had to be an informer in the doctor's house, or this imaginative gambit would never have been checkmated. But it was.

Lille doctors had come under close surveillance when one was unwittingly betrayed by his maid. After she was found crying during a routine police visit, she explained naïvely that her master's son had just been killed at Arras. Since this engagement was but a day old, the Germans knew that the doctor or one of his staff was either linked to the resistance or subscribed to one of the forbidden newspapers. Just to be sure, the doctor was shipped off to a prison hospital in Germany for the duration.

In the same class was the not entirely unique attempt at transporting intelligence within artificial eyes. Soon, counterintelligence was shining flashlights into the faces of any suspected courier. The pupil which did not at once contract under the bright beam was obviously a false one.

By the same token, it became routine that any person with a wooden leg, a man or a woman, would have to unhook it when passing a control point. If it were hollow, which most were, it would then have to be upended and shaken vigorously. Some very compromising documents occasionally fluttered down from the artificial limbs.

Messages also found their way into hollowed-out shoe heels or beneath the plasters over nonexistent wounds. Before long, bandages, legitimate or not, were being torn off travelers with ruthless abandon. Umbrellas and walking canes, too, were chopped into kindling, just in case.

The sometimes imitative Prussian mind copied one ruse to fatal disadvantage: removing half the lead from pencils and then pushing a tightly rolled message inside the wood. A suspected enemy agent, detained near Ypres, was about to be freed when a casual clerk in the local French Deuxieme (intelligence) Bureau became curious as to why the man carried so many lead pencils.

Carefully, the clerk weighed each pencil on an apothecary scale. When he came upon one relatively lighter than the others, he cracked it open and discovered on neatly folded tissue paper the diagram of the Third Canadian Brigade's artillery defenses. Thus, the Kaiser lost, forever, the services of one more agent.

Food, too, tended to be a favorite means of disguising messages. Louise once watched bemused as a border police-man sliced into thin wafers a sausage she was carrying in her purse. He ignored the compartments of the purse itself, containing incriminating messages, tossed boldly onto the inspector's desk.

Another time, Louise wrapped a pair of disreputable old shoes in a mussed brown paper which actually presented a mosaic in invisible ink of gun emplacement plans for the Fourth and Sixth German armies. Their logistics were centered primarily in the Lille area. Frontier guards were wholly uninterested in this unsavory-appearing bundle.

These gleanings funneled through Louise's house, or that of Leonie, had to be assembled in a blacked-out, curtained room, lit only by a small, flickering candle, in defiance of the nightly curfew. All Lille citizens were supposed to be in bed and asleep, or at least not sitting up trying to outwit the conqueror.

These dark, silent hours were especially peril-frought, since Captain Himmel was relentlessly pursuing a regular block search. A square area of Lille was marked off each night for a systematic and ruthless scouring. The occupant could not anticipate what was going to happen until the door crashed open, followed by the guttural: "Raus! Raus!" In this brusque fashion, the secret police ransacked a hundred or more houses every night. Nor could the resident breathe a sigh of relief when the Germans left. They might return to the identical block the following night.

While Louise drew no distinction between peddler or preacher, store clerk or bureaucrat, male or female in selecting couriers, she abandoned the use of young people after Leon Trulin was executed. The seventeen-year-old Lille boy had made three successful trips to the Netherlands border and was about to enlist in the French Army when betrayed.

The night before he was to be shot in the Citadel, Leon wrote to his mother:

"I beseech you not to despair . . . I embrace you with all my heart. Courage, mother, we shall see each other again someday. Kiss my brother and sisters for me and tell them your son knew how to die. . . .

"I forgive everybody, friends and enemies I pardon because they do not pardon me. . . .

"Your son who causes you much suffering and is deeply grieved . . ."

Impassioned protests from the clergy of the twelfth-century Church of St. Christopher were to no avail. Trulin, refusing to have his eyes bandaged, died.

The next day, the Germans drilled behind a blaring army band in the Grande Place. Staffs and patrons alike of the overlooking Hotel Cygne, with its huge swan sign, and the adjacent Café Moderne stayed behind drawn blinds, ignor-

ing the insolent conqueror in one of the few expressions
permitted them.

Several days later, the injured feelings of the populace
were in no degree assuaged when the Kaiser himself, passing
through the city, reviewed goose-stepping platoons in front
of the crumbling façade of the Gare Centrale.

The Alice Service's spiriting of Allied soldiers or young
Frenchmen across the border also was dealt a severe blow
when Eugene Jacquet, a wine merchant, and three others
were executed for aiding a British aviator, Lieutenant Cyril
Mapplebeck, to escape. Mapplebeck had been shot down
while attempting to drop Paris newspapers in aluminum
crates and carrier pigeons to Louise's colleagues. This expedient for winging intelligence back to the Allies was later
halted when it was found that the enemy was capturing
these birds and afixing compromising messages of their
own.

Before he was wholly clear of Lille, Mapplebeck, a jaunty,
devil-may-care aviator in the tradition of his flying corps,
posted a taunting letter to the German governor:

"Lieutenant Mapplebeck sends his compliments to the
Kommandant of the German forces in Lille and regrets that
he was unable to make his acquaintance during his recent
pleasant stay in the neighborhood!"

The postscript, to be emblazoned in blood by the Germans,
was not so funny: an "Avis" tacked on walls and bulletin
boards throughout Lille announcing that the four patriots
had been shot.

Yet more important to the Allies, however, than hustling
young men, soldiers, or aviators through the lines was the
patient gathering of information on German troop trains.
Their volume, frequency, and direction were of gold-plated
value.

Among Louise's more efficient harvesters of these vital facts and figures was a young wine vendor, Paul Provoust, of Courtrai. His clandestine correspondence was frequently passed on its rambling route by old, veiled ladies over holy water basins of churches.

"A battalion reduced to 500 men arrived here on the 1st," was typical of his intelligence reports. "Grey caps, blue border, black and white badges, red-piped shoulder straps. Very tired and dispirited. Came from Messines sector. Expected reinforcements had not arrived this morning when they left for Wytechaete. The anti-aircraft battery by the bridge has been enlarged by one gun."

Provoust had learned this while selling wine through parked troop trains and asking seemingly innocent questions, a bit at a time, of the soldiers.

"Why aren't you with your regiment?" he might ask casually, hoping to catch the soldier unawares. Of course, the wine vendor had no idea whether the trooper was with his regiment or not. If he were, the unit was no doubt on the move, and Provoust's next question, to someone in the next car, would attempt to elicit to which sector the regiment was being shunted.

Supplies and reinforcements for the Fourth and Sixth German armies rumbled day-long and all the night, with shaded locomotive lights, through the Roubaix-Mauveaux yards, fifteen miles northeast of Lille. The trains were rolling in from Courtrai and the east.

It was not enough merely to listen to the shrilling of whistles or report "great activity" in the huge marshaling yards. The count of cars and direction of enemy movements by rail had to be more exact. And this was not easy because the Germans also were aware of the importance *their* enemies attached to the railroads. Roubaix as well as nearby

Tourcoing seethed with counterspies and agents *provocateurs*.

One answer to this problem Louise de Bettignies found in the faded pre-Victorian home of a respected woman of Mauveaux, Mme. Elise-Julie Leveugle, permitted by the occupation troops to dispense charity to the needy. Her house not only was the focus of many callers but was next to the railroad yards.

All day she sat by her window, knitting, talking with an unending line of visitors—but, at the same time, counting every car, every locomotive. Between knocks upon her door she would make little notes of these numbers, with a hint as to the type of train and, if she could see, who were riding behind the half-shuttered car windows.

At night, she rocked in the blackness of her room and continued to count. So that no time would be lost, she recorded the totals by tapping her heel upon the floor. Her son in the room immediately below kept a running tally. If there were urgency, he would leave stealthily with the information for Mme. Leveugle's immediate "letter box" in the Alice Service.

One acquaintance, Pierre Coulson, a lifelong tobacconist, managed to obtain a stationmaster's appointment at one of these listening posts, a junction outlying Roubaix. Compensating for lack of technical qualifications by his friendly wit, he would edge up to a German railroad guard, usually an old soldier from the reserve regiments, a *Landstürmer*, then confess:

"I'm fed up around here! It's bad enough to be awakened at night for a house search, but to have you fellows spying on me all day long . . ."

Often the guard would relax and complain of his own sore

feet, his schmerz or soul-weariness over military authority, and, customarily, a gnawing homesickness for his own little *haus* in Bavaria. Then, he might add, with no idea of the compromising value:

". . . and all the trains I have to watch. Mein Gott, there were sixteen today going toward Cambrai alone!"

Coulson sometimes hid under small bridges at night and estimated the length of the trains by the clicks of the wheels over one track joint. He divided by two to obtain the car count—mathematics of the most elemental kind.

Enemy rail operations remained of paramount interest to the Allies. In fact, as 1915 wore out, the sum total of the Alice Service intelligence concerning trains moving through the great Lille complex began to add up to one inescapable conclusion: the enemy was massing his forces to the south.

Early in 1916, this information was evaluated alongside reports of many other trains clattering west through Luxembourg. Deserters said the Seventh Reserve Corps was filing into Verdun. This citadel town, 150 miles south of Lille, guarded the flat plains—a well-trodden invasion route—leading to Paris.

Thus, when the blow fell on Verdun, February 21, 1916, the Crown Prince himself could not wholly understand why the French defenders had not been taken by surprise.

Perhaps her part in anticipating Verdun, which was to bleed both antagonists white, was justification enough for Louise de Bettignies' work within the German zone of occupation. At any rate, emboldened by her successes, she violated a cardinal rule of her profession—she grew careless.

"Oh, they are too stupid to catch *us!*" she boasted to Leonie.

In August and September, German counterintelligence

was arresting patriots wantonly in Belgium. Two of them were Louise's best couriers, Louise Thuliez,* a Lille school-teacher, and Princess Marie de Croy, who hid men in her château.

On August 5, a woman not engaged in espionage, but deeply committed to smuggling escaped prisoners of war and young Belgians across the border, was betrayed and jailed: a forty-nine-year-old English nurse, Edith Cavell, who was directress of a nurses' school and private hospital, the Depage Clinic, in Brussels.

On September 24, Leonie "Charlotte" was arrested at a Brussels rendezvous, the Hotel St. Jean. She at once ate several rice paper messages hidden in her clothing. It was not soon enough to save her from imprisonment. And the luck even of Mme. de Geyter ran out. This time she could not talk her way to freedom.

Captain Himmel's agents reasoned that Leonie van Houtte possessed intimate knowledge of the entire resistance in northeast France. But they had no idea of her stubbornness.

"Louise *who?*" she would reply blandly. Or, "Alice who?" if they inquired about Alice Dubois.

Leonie could be master of what French writers would describe as *"le silence heroique des condemnés!"*

She alternated this silence with bland questions which seemed to hint at no knowledge of any given subject, and occasional meandering answers loaded with false information or at best misleading half-truths.

The Alice Service, however, could no longer be held together, no matter the courage and stoicism of "Charlotte."

---

* Louise Thuliez was unvanquished by the Germans, however, and died in Paris in October, 1966.

Orders flashed in from Berlin to Baron Moritz von Bissing, the military governor of Belgium, to stamp out civilian resistance or disobedience of any degree without restraint or mercy. The aging officer, a retired general who had seen action in the Franco-Prussian War, then summoned his Judge Advocate, a younger man with a frozen face beneath straight tuftings of hair fiercely greased and parted in the middle: Dr. Stoeber, already infamous as a "hanging judge." The sobriquet had not been idly earned.

Stoeber promised Von Bissing he would set "a horrible example!" when he started his trials.

By the time Leonie was apprehended, the prosecutor had arrested nearly one hundred Belgians and French citizens, men and women. Thirty-five were actually brought to trial and most of them given ample prison sentences "at hard labor." However, all but two of the death sentences were commuted.

On October 12, Edith Cavell died at the Tir National, a former Belgian army rifle range, in Brussels. At her side was an otherwise obscure Belgian architect, Philippe Baucq— not accorded lighter punishment, some theorized, because the German mind, in its unfathomable sense of right and wrong and martial jurisprudence, could not, of all paradoxes, countenance the prospect of a woman being led to execution alone.

Just a week later, Louise, hurrying to Brussels, possibly to try to repair the shattered lines of communication, was arrested at the border. Her contempt for the capabilities of the Germans this time was her undoing. Her purse, crammed with forged ID cards for members of her "service," omitted her own.

Handcuffed to an Abteilung agent, she was hurried to

Brussels in the curtained compartment of a Wagons Lits railroad car. Once in the Belgian capital Louise was taken to St. Gilles Prison, an especially huge institution built on the pattern of wheel spokes.

Louise occupied a small cell only a few doors removed from one relinquished just the previous week by the martyred Edith Cavell. And next to this newest woman prisoner was a twenty-three-year-old Molenbeek, Belgium, girl: Gabrielle Petit. She was awaiting trial on charges of treason.

Well-known to Louise de Bettignies, for both her schoolgirl beauty and daring, Gabrielle was engaged to be married at the time of the German invasion. When her fiancé was killed, Gabrielle submerged herself in the service of her country. She was, for a time, courier for the forbidden unique letter-publication, "Le Mot du Soldat," through which families were able to learn of their sons, fathers, and brothers at the front.

At Lille, early in the great conflict, Gabrielle had nearly been caught in a hotel requisitioned for officers. Hiding under the eaves in the chambermaids' quarters, Gabrielle was awakened by a determined pounding on the door.

She knew there could be but two reasons for male visitors at this hour: Captain Himmel's police or some drunken Oberst. She did not wait to find out which. Throwing an overcoat over her nightclothes, the fleet-footed girl jumped into her boots and leaped through a back window onto a fire escape. She raced down the shaky old steps to the cobblestoned alley. Gabrielle then hid out in Mme. Leveugle's home until she considered it safe once more to make for the border.

Her useful career was brought to an abrupt end and through betrayal by an all too common and also effective gambit in the secret war. Abteilung agents, posing as Frenchmen with enemy fortification diagrams for sale, were directed to the home of the young woman's aunt in Brussels where she was staying for a few days.

Although suspicious, Gabrielle negotiated for the plans— and was arrested. Tried and convicted of "treason," a curious charge against a patriot in her own country, Gabrielle was sentenced to death by a firing squad.

As in the case of Edith Cavell, none thought the Germans would actually go through with this barbarism. And so Gabrielle waited in her cell at St. Gilles.

Meanwhile, the secret police, unable to decide whether Louise of Lille was actually a De Bettignies or Alice Dubois, tried to resolve their quandry by rounding up everyone in Brussels named "Dubois." There were hundreds: male and female, girls and boys, young and old. Some came into the headquarters at 24 Rue de Berlaimont on crutches; others, aged and infirm, were carried or assisted by stronger kinfolk.

Each was asked to account for everything he or she did, every place visited for the past several months. Finally, submerged under a mountain of the most banal trivia and worthless affidavits, the Germans disgustedly threw away the whole dossier, certain at least that the woman in St. Gilles Prison was *not* Alice Dubois, if indeed such a person truly did exist.

Louise continued to thwart, mislead, tease, occasionally mimic but always harass her captors. Prosecutor Stoeber himself kept the trial under way only with difficulty.

"Speak French, monsieur," Louise would request, with extravagant politeness. Then, when the prosecutor had strug-

gled through minutes of very bad French, she would unexpectedly reply in faultless German.

"Ah!" Stoeber might exclaim in relief. "So we may talk my
language, after all?"

"Certainly not," the pretty defendant would answer,
demurely. "The law specifies that any prisoner must be addressed in his own language so that the nature of the charges
may be fully understood."

And so the trial went, with interpreters grudgingly paid
for by the German prosecution. At one time, hoping to trick
information out of her, Louise's captors placed an informer
in her cell, who called herself Louise Tellier. Her accent
gave her away.

Louise annoyed the military, as well, by her contemptuous indifference toward her own defense. She did, however,
make a plea for Leonie, "because she is so young and has so
much of her life yet to live!"

Mlle. van Houtte was spared, although her sentence was
not light: fifteen years at hard labor. On the same day,
March 19, 1916, Louise was sentenced to death.

Not quite two weeks later, early on the morning of April 1,
prisoners in the women's row of St. Gilles heard the voice of
Gabrielle Petit, loudly singing:

"Salut o mon dernier matin . . . !"

She was telling of her "last morning." Gabrielle had not
deceived her comrades.

And so the brave Mlle. Petit, of Molenbeek, joined Edith
Cavell, Leon Trulin, Eugene Jacquet—a growing multitude
of citizens of France, Belgium, and Britain who had paid
with their lives for defying the despot.

The Germans would never learn. They must have read, for
example, that upward of 100,000 young Englishmen had

flocked to recruiting stations in the fortnight following the shooting of Miss Cavell, who, as Gabrielle, had "taught men how to die."

In Trafalgar Square, men signed up for "the forces" beneath a huge and challenging sign:

"WHO'LL AVENGE NURSE CAVELL?"

Marshal Foch, touched but not entirely surprised at Louise de Bettignies' sentence of death, conferred upon her *in absentia* the *Ordre de l'Armes*, declaring that she possessed "a heroism rarely surpassed . . . inflexible courage."

Louise wrote farewell to her mother, concluding, "*à Dieu, Ma Mère!*"

Mercy remained, as before, not among the Kaiser's notable indulgences. However, a hint of the worldwide outrage still mounting over the slaughter of civilians, especially civilian women, began to penetrate even Emperor Wilhelm's thick skull. Louise's sentence was commuted to life imprisonment.

She was moved to a German women's prison at Siegburg, near Cologne, overlooking the Rhine River. Along with three hundred others, Louise endured confinement: small, cold cells, never enough food nor warm clothing. Nonetheless, although she sickened, her spirit did not waver.

She inspired protests of many sorts. She adamantly refused to work in munitions plants, as other women prisoners had been required to do.

The months dragged on.

The Alice Service was dead. But its seeds were fertile. Successors, organized by the British and French secret services and by patriots in occupied towns and provinces, grew up in its place. There was, notably, the Service Michelin, renamed shortly the unimaginative B-149 and, finally, with unusual suggestive éclat, "The White Lady." Like the Alice Service, it paid dearly for its work.

The names of the women continued to take their places in honor beside those of their male comrades who fell before German firing squads: Elise Grandprez, Emilie Schattemann, Leonia Rammeloo, others who sacrificed their lives for the cause of "The White Lady." The Kaiser never would learn his lesson.

Yet, harshness, impersonality, and sudden death were not wholly partial to any one warring side. The fury of war once unleashed did not burn itself out overnight, or in many nights. And, like a maniac with fire, it was careless.

Woodrow Wilson himself understood with crystal clarity what war meant. He had confided his own apocalypse, almost in anguish, to a newspaper friend the very night before his war message to Congress:

"Once lead this people into war and they'll forget there ever was such a thing as tolerance. To fight you must be brutal and ruthless, and the spirit of ruthless brutality will enter into the very fibre of our national life. . . ."

It was true in all of the warring countries. Only the degree, frequency, and manner differed. Civilization took great steps backward—everywhere. On October 15, 1917, executed near Paris was Dutch-born Margarete Zelle-better known as the exotic dancer "Mata Hari," meaning in Javanese, "Eye of the Dawn." She was a dumpy, rather weary forty-one.

Mata Hari had studied at the German spy school at Lorrach in 1914. Among valuable information she had conveyed to Berlin was the news that the British were fabricating a *Landschiffe* or "land ship," the tank. She was captured en route from Madrid back to Paris. In her luggage was an incriminating supply of francs, furnished her through the *Nachrichtendienst.*

The French prosecution claimed that "at least 50,000 French soldier deaths" could be attributed directly to Mata Hari's intelligence. This probably was court-martial showmanship, but she had been an effective agent, anyhow.

The "Eye of the Dawn" expired in a dank French dawn, at suburban Vincennes. The few witnesses present were to report with a measure of surprise that she went bravely, refusing a blindfold, in the best traditions of a hazardous profession.

It was an unthinking observation. Women, spies or nonspies, have always died bravely.

Louise de Bettignies' condition meanwhile worsened. All prison cells were solitary so far as roommates went. However, Leonie and a few other prisoners, including Louise Thuliez, who had been sentenced at the same time as Edith Cavell, were allowed to care for her.

Finally, when nothing more could be done within the walls of the fortress-prison, Louise was removed to a nearby convent. There an operation for what was perhaps incorrectly diagnosed as pleurisy was performed.

The operating room was makeshift, the surgeon's instruments and general surroundings far from aseptic. Louise survived the butchery, but not for long. She succumbed on September 17, 1918.

The Armistice was less than two months distant.

Posthumously, Louise de Bettignies was awarded the Croix de Guerre. Other of Lille's heroes and martyrs were also remembered. Eugene Jacquet, for example, who had aided the English aviator to escape, posthumously was decorated with the Knight of the Legion of Honor.

In London, an official of the secret service extolled Louise's "inestimable" contributions.

"Through her," he declared, "we learned with a precision, a regularity and rapidity that was never surpassed by any other organization all the movements of the enemy, the exact position of their batteries and 1,000 details that were of great help to our headquarters. . . . we admired, almost revered the young French girl. We adored her . . . !"

If her captors did not precisely "adore" Louise de Bettignies, they demonstrated heavy-handedly their regard for her. Her coffin was zinc-lined, an extravagance unheard of because of the scarcity of all metals.

The Armistice Commission and the Red Cross located her grave that same winter. Her exhumation, anticipated by the Germans, was arranged.

While sleet fell through the almost deserted streets of Cologne, now just another city in a defeated nation, Louise's casket, draped with her country's Tricolor, was drawn on a gun carriage between an honor guard of stiffly marching British and French soldiers. The roll of muffled drums which sounded their funeral adieus at the smoky old Kölnischer Bahnhof was picked up again in the streets of Lille, no less gray than Cologne at this time of year.

All that was mortal of "Alice Dubois" was laid to rest on March 4, 1919, in St. Amand Cemetery. She was accorded full military honors, concluding as always with the rifles' final salute—rolling over the flower mounds and the fresh-spaded dirt, echoing through the yet gaunt ruins of Lille, fading into silence.

It seemed that an era as well as a heady way of life had been interred with Louise forever. And a next day's headline in the *Paris Herald* eloquently underscored how rapidly the war and all it had been or implied in its countless innuendoes was slipping inexorably into the void of yesterday:

JAZZ AND TICKLE-TOE
FEVER RAMPANT IN LONDON

"London is dancing," the dispatch read, "Paris is dancing, the whole world is dancing because the war is over."

An almost infinitesimal segment of the world, however, called for intermission in its gyrations long enough to reflect upon the leader of the Alice Service. The newspaper *l'Echo de Paris*, along with the United Veterans Association of France and the Association of Political Prisoners of Toulon, launched a fund to erect a statue in her memory.

In February, 1927, a bronze plaque was nailed onto the Bettignies house on the Rue d'Isly, Lille. In November, the statue, finally ready, was dedicated in a small square at the entrance to the Boulevard de la Republique.

Marie Leonie van Houtte and the aging Mme. Mabille de Bettignies were honored guests.

A few weeks later Louise's mother was dead. Marie was swallowed up once more in the anonymity of the shops of Roubaix—forever so far as the world beyond the town's cobblestones and terra cotta rooftops would ever know.

The dancing, singing, the drinking, the forgetting, continued for a far shorter period than even the most pessimistic had predicted. The strains of the *Marsellaise* which had sounded at the dedication of Louise's statue and the volleys which had cracked over her grave that blustery March morning would echo again two decades later.

Lille became the "cradle of the resistance" in a France

subjugated by the Germans for the second time in less than half a century. The city's wartime role was not without precedent.

The stouthearted inhabitants were branded by their conquerors as "truculent" even before the Vichy capitulation. They worked in factories for the Nazis only at gunpoint. They did everything to obstruct and retard the enemy's operations.

Once again, the rail yards became a focus of interest. This time, loaded trains, freight sheds, and long sections of track were blown up by the *Maquis*. New names took their place beside Lilles immortals of the first World War: Max Leroux, Jules, Sylvestre, "Yolande," and preeminently Michel Trotobas, a legend in his own time who singlehandedly fought nearly a score of SS troopers, "Hitler's Own," before he fell.

And so another war was repeating the same sordid story of man's folly and unreasoning cruelty. He was saved from abject hopelessness only by acts of bravery and heroism to a degree seldom attained in peacetime. Woman's measure of these ultimates proved to be on the increase.

4

⁜

THE KAISER'S WOMAN IN NEW YORK
⋯► *Maria de Victorica, 1918*

While Louise and those who followed her were frustrating
the Prussian conqueror, spying jumped the Atlantic Ocean
to become a part of America's vicarious preoccupations, tea-
time conversations, and, with the queasy, haunting night-
mares.

"Spies," screamed the New York *Tribune*, "are everywhere! They occupy hundreds of observation posts. They
are in the Army and Navy. They are going freely to and fro.
They are in factories producing war materials. They are in
all the drug and chemical laboratories."

Senator Benjamin R. "Pitchfork Ben" Tillman, of South
Carolina, stormily seconding the *Tribune*'s suspicions and
charges, urged that these spies be ferreted out of the War
and Navy Departments so they could be "hanged or shot."
His was not the only excited congressional voice.

The otherwise conservative *Literary Digest* added som-
berly that ninety spies had been arrested and interned in the
last week of September, 1917, alone, "some of whom had in

their possession plans and even finished parts of a new
American invention described as 'one of the most destructive
agencies of war yet evolved by American genius.' Berlin may
even now know all about it. . . ."

The Syracuse *Herald* observed bitterly that no other country in the world offered a climate so "healthful and salubri-
ous" for foreign agents. Pointing to the "extremely low
mortality rate" of persons in this profession in America, the
upstate New York daily deplored: "We haven't hanged or
shot any spies yet, [but] we have reprimanded some very
severely."

The Providence *Journal* somewhat later asserted: "It
seems preposterous to talk about driving the Kaiser back
across the Rhine when we do not drive off his American
army which reports its victories to Berlin in every issue of
the American newspapers."

Other writers related a $43 million fire loss in factories
identified with "war industries" to the "American army" of
Kaiser Wilhelm. While some, most notably the Black Tom
munitions pier explosion in the summer of 1916, were unquestionably of sabotage or arsonist origin, the accident
rate, through the carelessness of unskilled wartime labor,
was a very strong but overlooked factor.

An "On Your Guard Movement," started by the Fifth
Avenue Association of New York, quickly spread to more
than one hundred cities across the nation. Citizenry were
exhorted to be on the *qui vive* for words or actions of any
sort which might "weaken patriotic energy."

The fever attacked high-placed victims.

"We found," observed T. W. Gregory, Attorney General
of the United States, "our soil to be infected with representatives of an unscrupulous power which did not hesitate to

violate our hospitality and break its most sacred pledges in using this country as a base for unneutral plots against France and Great Britain."

The sinking of the *Lusitania* on May 27, 1915, inspired a geyser of rumors, including those about secret wireless stations on Long Island, black touring cars carrying moustached passengers speeding through Central Park in the dead of night, and, of course, women in tight satin dresses, smoking cigarettes out of long-stemmed holders. All of the femmes fatales, somehow, were assumed to have insinuated themselves into society's parapets, like beautiful but strangling vines.

These were unfortunate and frequently perilous times in which to "look German" or to have been born with a German or even "foreign" sounding name. Arrests of suspected spies mounted until soon *The New York Times,* hard-pressed to keep up with the volume of individual reportings, was running indexes several columns long under two distinct categories. One was headed "Alien Plotters and Agitators," the other more succinctly "Spies."

Charges, if any, tended to be vague: "walking near a munitions plant [or Army post, a reservoir, or even a bridge]" "carrying a camera," "associating with aliens," "loitering," the old local police precinct standby, "on suspicion," or "for investigation."

Bird watchers themselves became fair game. With their binoculars, cameras, and affinity for wandering wide-eyed, about lonely areas, they could not help but attract attention. Many of them decided it was prudent to put away the symbols of their avocation for the duration and remain close to home.

A dispatch from a small Iowa town soberly reported the

arrest of one "Blowupsky." Naturally, he was also carrying a black, heavy, round-shaped parcel. Other such implausible names found their way, if not onto police dossiers, into print.

Off Manhattan Beach, Long Island, three men quietly fishing in their rowboat were suddenly swooped upon by a Coast Guard cutter and dragged to shore under heavy guard. The cause of their apprehension: the trio happened to have been anchored over a cable crossing.

The generally more realistic *Ladies' Home Journal* went to press with an article, "The Way the Spy Works," and citizens of all ages who lived near the East Coast were urged to be "on the lookout for pigeons or seagulls that come in exhausted or seem tame." Such birds were to be suspect of having winged across the Atlantic Ocean, all the way from Berlin.

There were some "birds" up to no good, and their number included Captain Franz von Papen and Captain Karl Boy-Ed, the military and naval attachés, respectively, at the German embassy, who were "invited" to return home twenty months before America's entry into the war. Dr. Constantin Dumba, Austrian ambassaor to the United States, was also sent packing.

Count Johann Friedrich von Bernstorff, the German ambassador, was allowed to remain until shortly before Congress' declaration of war in April, 1917. In his subsequent memoirs, von Bernstorff, reemphasizing earnestly his own desires to maintain America's neutrality, disavowed any liaison with the plotters.

He might well have. Much of their cabals and intrigue were of the substance of comic opera. Von Papen and Boy-Ed were revealed as especially fun-loving emissaries when

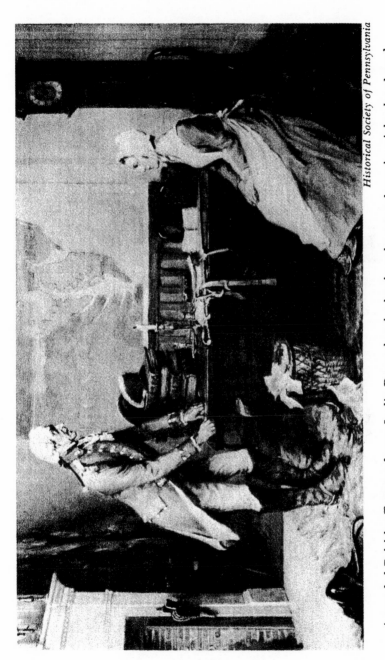

A puzzled British officer confronts Lydia Darragh, who he thought was asleep the night she alerted Washington to the enemy's plans. Painting by John Ward Dunsmore. (Chapter 1)

Lydia Darragh, the little Quaker woman, became an ancestral patron of American female spies when she walked out of the Loxley House in Philadelphia to carry tidings to General Washington. (Chapter 1)

General John Hunt Morgan, who underestimated the power of a woman spy. (Chapter 2)

Belle Boyd spent so much of the Civil War years in Federal prisons that she had scant time for the spying she reputedly carried on for the Confederacy. (Chapter 2)

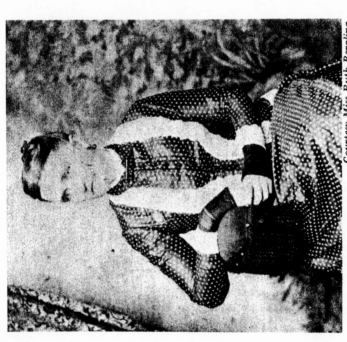

Courtesy Miss Ruth Bergling

Sarah Thompson, taken at about the time she betrayed the presence of General John Hunt Morgan to the Federal troops. (Chapter 2)

Treasury Department,
OFFICE OF THE SECRETARY.

January 29, 1879.

Mrs S. E. Thompson
Office of the Second Auditor. Defunct.
Madam:

You are informed that by reason of the exhaustion of the fund from which you have been paid the Department is unable to continue your services from and after the 30th instant.

Very respectfully,
John Sherman
Secretary.

Letter informing Sarah Thompson that she is dismissed by the Treasury Department for lack of funds. (Chapter 2)

BEWARE

— OF —

FEMALE SPIES

Women are being employed by the enemy to secure information from Navy men, on the theory that they are less liable to be suspected than male spies. Beware of inquisitive women as well as prying men.

SEE EVERYTHING
HEAR EVERYTHING
SAY NOTHING

Concerning any matter bearing upon the work of the Navy

SILENCE IS SAFETY

LEFT: World War I poster. (Chapter 3) RIGHT: French hostages at Lille during World War I shown in a drawing by a German artist, Fritz Erler, belying Germany's denial that hostages such as these were taken and shot. (Chapter 3)

Louise de Bettignies, the French heroine who inaugurated the "Alice Service" in World War I. (Chapter 3)

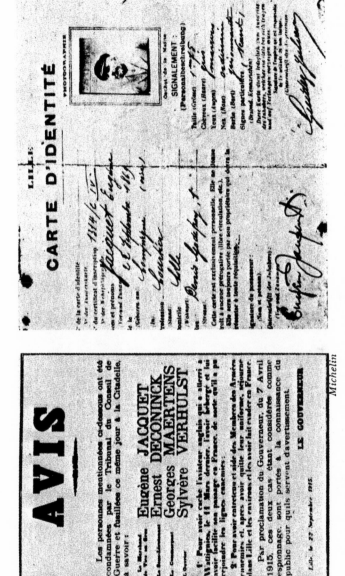

Michelin

When the Germans executed civilians, they posted notices for all to read. These four citizens of Lille were shot in September for assisting the escape of an English aviator. (Chapter 3) This typical identity card in Lille during the German occupation in the first World War belonged to Eugene Jacquet who was executed. (Chapter 3)

Eastman Kodak Company

Kodak Girls, reproduced from a 1914 advertising postcard. It was a Kodak girl, Mena Edwards, who reported to the Justice Department that she was a friend of Captain Franz von Papen, then the military attaché at the German embassy. (Chapter 4)

The I. D. card of Violette Szabo. Her first mission for the British SOE (Special Operations Executive) in France was successful. Her second, later in 1944, led to her capture and execution. She was awarded posthumously the George Cross, Britain's highest civilian honor. (Chapter 6)

Diana Rowden, a twenty-nine year old yachting enthusiast who accompanied Noor Inayat Khan to France and was executed at Natzweiler extermination camp. (Chapter 6)

Vera Leigh, a forty-one year old dress designer who was executed at Himmler's command with a deadly injection of phenol. (Chapter 6)

Noor Inayat Khan, who operated a clandestine radio station in the shadow of Gestapo headquarters and was shot at Dachau prison. (Chapter 6)

Odette Marie Sansom (now Mrs. Geoffrey Hallowes) who was tortured by the Gestapo rather than reveal information they sought, and received the George Cross for her bravery. (Chapter 6)

Courtesy Barbara Wheeler

Barbara Slade, (now Mrs. Allen H. Wheeler) the young lady who identified the German V-1 flying bomb site ready for firing. (Chapter 8)

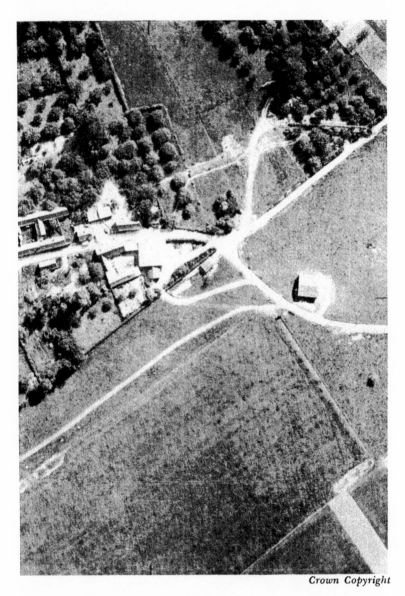

An aerial photograph of a Belhamelin-type launching site with the firing rail up. (Chapter 8)

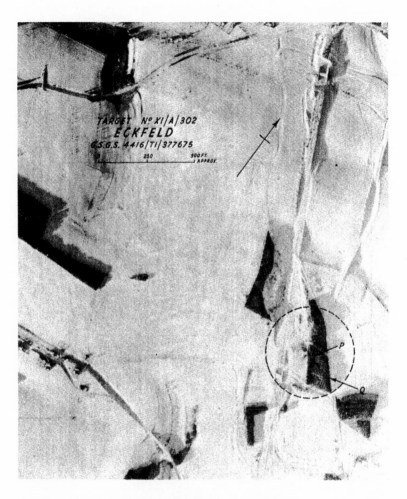

TARGET № XI/A/302
ECKFELD
G.S.G.S. 4416/TI/377675

A German "Diver" flying bomb site is analyzed from an aerial photograph. "The ramp [marked 'P'] is situated in the edge of a wood and fires across a cutting for the unfinished Cologne-Trier Autobahn. A building probably the Square Building (Q) is behind the ramp in direct line with it." (Chapter 8)

Milada Horakava, the brave resistance leader who fought the Nazi occupation of her native Czechoslovakia only to be executed for her challenge to the Communist domination of her country. (Chapter 9)

one of their friends, Mena Edwards, the "Eastman Girl," decided to talk.

Mena, the curvaceous model for Kodak advertisements, volunteered to the Justice Department that she and her roommate Martha Heldt (sometimes "Martha Gordon") had been to countless parties with the diplomats: at the German Club, at the Ritz, Delmonico's, and other places of assignation including the attachés' uptown New York apartments. She tried to recall snatches of conversation or hints of "plots" from their playful soirées. About all, however, that could be safely deduced from her testimony was that the diplomats just liked women, beer, brandy, to sing the sentimental *lieder*, and, especially, to have a good time.

(Years later, Von Papen, in his memoirs, hotly denied even knowing the girls and was especially scornful of Mena's reminiscing of horseback gallops in Central Park. An accomplished rider, however, the German officer gave this interesting rebuttal, "the horse I hired from the Central Park Riding Academy loathed other horses and always had to be ridden alone.")

This *Gemütlichkeit* was abruptly terminated after Von Papen was sent home and then ordered to active service in the army, partly no doubt because of the embarrassments he caused during his tour of duty in America. After fighting bravely on the Somme front, he was assigned as Chief of Staff to the Fourth Turkish Army, in Palestine, under General Liman von Sanders.

He had been better off at the western front, where others could keep an eye on him. One cold night, a surprise raid by the Australians projected this moustached, rather ferociously handsome officer into a new contretemps of buffoonery. Clad only in his ankle-length sleeping gown, Von

Papen fled from his tent into the desert, barefooted, leaving codes and secret documents behind in his tent. To their unbridled amusement, the Aussies read the German warning pasted atop the strongbox:

"Burn—if danger of seizure!"

From Allied headquarters in Alexandria came a historic, bemused order: "If Von Papen captured, don't send him to prison, but to a lunatic asylum!"

(Perhaps he should have been sent somewhere, since unfortunately the inept plotter of the first World War was destined to leave a larger, and blacker mark in German hanky-panky. He served six months as Chancellor of the new Reich, before relinquishing the all-important post to Adolf Hitler's National Socialists. Subsequently, he softened up Austria for *Anschluss* and later managed a listening post during World War II in Ankara. His life was fantastically charmed. He escaped assassination at least twice and was among the few connected with the July, 1944, bomb plot against the Fuehrer, to be overlooked during the mass reprisals. He was one of only three to be found not guilty at the Nuremberg trials, although a German de-Nazification court sent him to prison for eight years as a leading Nazi. Von Papen lives today in southern Germany, aged, unwell, but nonetheless a notable exception to the rule that there are bold spies and old spies, but rarely old, bold spies.)

Von Papen and Boy-Ed had dual instructions, to foment anti-American feeling in Mexico and to organize a saboteur ring in New York for placing bombs on outgoing French and British freighters. Their successor, Captain Franz von Rintelen, a naval officer, proved more professional, although he too was caught. He admitted to having secreted some thirty-two pencil-shaped incendiary bombs on Europe-bound ships. Von Rintelen spent his confinement at the Federal Penitentiary in Atlanta railing at the "common criminals" who were his cell neighbors.

A second-rate agent, Werner Horn, was seized attempting to blow up a railroad bridge leading from Vanceboro, Maine, to New Brunswick. This dull-witted bungler was saved from a Canadian hangman by all-forgiving American authorities who refused to extradite him.

Arrested on more interesting if not necessarily more incriminating specifications was Bruno von Bultzingsloven, described as the inventor of a flying machine which he called the "aeromobile." The German-born New York resident was charged on a federal warrant with confiding unwittingly to a counteragent, working for the Department of Justice, "everything is fair in war—gas, poison, the bomb and the knife. We must stop at nothing. The object justifies the means, and the object is Germany's triumph over her enemies, who want to wipe her out, I have never yet killed anybody but I wouldn't hesitate to destroy a whole city for the good of the German cause."

His neighbors in the Bronx hitherto had the notion that Von Bultzingsloven was merely a harmless, past middle-age eccentric who drank too much beer and spoke too little English. No one had ever seen his "aeromobile."

Werner Horn, as well as the thwarted inventor, had plenty of company on a scrub team which proved to be a motley assortment of consolation-prize agents, alleged agents, or would-be agents skulking across the pages of American newspapers and sometimes even onto police blotters. Their very names, which often connoted darkness and furtive conspiracy, tended to be more impressive and conceivably more sinister than their deeds: Franz Bopp, Horst von der Goltz,

Wolf von Igel, Albert Kaltschmidt, Johann H. von Koolbergen, Karl von Reiswitz, and many more.

These "arch-plotters," as they were flattered in print,
could hardly be whispered in the same breath with a Walsingham or a Schulmeister. Neither could the lesser number
of women who were identified with them or who were from
time to time arrested, abortively questioned, then released.

Of this mare's nest, Baroness Iona Zollner, of Chattanooga, sounded most likely as though she were a German
spy. At least, so casting her in a film would have seemed
appropriate. When it turned out that her husband was an
officer in the Kaiser's army, fighting in Flanders, that did it.
She was seized at her house, which was ransacked with the
meticulous detachment of a vacuum cleaner.

Sure enough, there was a letter to her son, also living in
the homeland, in which she alluded to a recent motor trip to
Fort Oglethorpe, Georgia. In it, she detailed the routes she
took, the conditions of the roads, where she stopped to eat,
the weather . . . Here, indeed, was a dangerous woman, a
twentieth-century Delilah who should be, and for a time
was, kept under lock and key.

These were days of especial uncertainty for boardinghouse keepers bearing German names. There were clusters
of them—houses and their owners—in many American
cities. Hoboken, a prewar port for scores of German liners,
now a snug harbor for their internment, was itself a Rhine-
land of German establishments and diluted culture, Amer-
ican-style.

One of Hoboken's number, Mrs. Anna Werner, came
under surveillance early in the war when it was whispered
that she sometimes went under an alias, Anna Herzog. This
happened to be her maiden name, but that obviously did not

forgive its use. Finally, she was arrested and her house ransacked down to and then under the moldings.

The detectives need not have gone to all the trouble. Right on her desk was a rough pencil sketch she had made of the Hudson River, while sitting on the broad lawns of nearby Stevens Institute. That any guidebook or penny postcard could furnish the same perspective and in consummately greater detail did not matter.

Across that river, in downtown Manhattan, an operator with the Postal Telegraph Company, Wanda Kreutzinger, forty-two, was also hauled in. Her name was just too German to satisfy the authorities. Besides, she had transmitted some telegrams to New Haven, Connecticut, an area known to be filled with "war" factories.

And there was a pretty twenty-two-year-old woman, Vara Margaret, whose only offense consisted of being married to a man charged with posing as an American Army officer in order to obtain military information.

However, there were also women possessing foreign names who were working for "our side." Mila Jerushkova, for one, a governess for a German widow in New York, faithfully reported visitors and conversations to the Army's MI-8, or newly informed intelligence service. The widow had some connection with Von Rintelen's destructively intentioned group.

After America's entry into the war, Mila agreed to be "deported" to Austria and continue her intelligence activities. Betrayed, however, she was tried in Prague and sentenced to death by hanging.

Von Bernstorff himself revealed a gallant spirit when he joined in an appeal for clemency which had originated in the

Vatican. Some of her snooping in New York had involved letters to and from the then German ambassador.

Whatever had influenced them, the authorities could not bring themselves to carry out the harsh sentence. But neither did they feel it appropriate to commute it. So Mila languished in her death cell, literally in the shadow of the gallows, nearly until the Armistice, when Austria-Hungary concluded its own peace with the Allies.

Pale, emaciated, she walked out into the blinding sunlight, at long last free. But she was a nervous wreck.

Mila had proved, among other things, that background and "foreign-sounding" names did not in themselves militate toward a person's spying for "the other side." Often it was a teeter-totter of fate that determined which combatant a secret operator would serve. And a few could not resist serving both, which made the game yet more exhilarating, one of double jeopardy. Then, too, the stakes were as high as mortally possible. The double spies were subject to being shot or hung by either side.

One woman, who because of her cosmopolitan background might as easily have served the Allied cause, chose nonetheless not to. She possessed a "class" and a culture quite unfamiliar to the German spies in America and became one of the more important ones.

She was Maria de Victorica, sometimes known as the Baroness Kretschmann, Marie de Vussiere, "the beautiful blonde of Antwerp," or just plain "Miss Clark." Actually, she was a light brunette, and not beautiful. She was plump, her features strongly Teutonic, "prepossessing" perhaps, but sternly handsome much as Rose Greenhow could be considered handsome.

Maria was born in Buenos Aires in 1882, the daughter of a

German Army officer who fought in the Franco-Prussian War. He called himself variously Captain, General, and, more often, Baron Hans von Kretschmann. He was but one of the rapidly expanding German colony of traders and exporters in South America. The Fatherland's flag had never before flown over so many far-flung consulates and embassies—and never would again. Her mother was the former Countess Jennie von Gustedt, related to the Kaiserin.

Like most of her predecessors, Maria left only a fragmentary autobiography for history to ponder. Fairly certainly she returned to Germany in her late teens for an education which, purportedly, commenced at Heidelberg and continued through the University of Berlin to the University of Zurich. At the completion of her considerable studies, which included political economy, she emerged as much of a linguist in her own right as Louise de Bettignies.

She apparently came into contact, possibly through friends in court circles who knew her mother or father, with Colonel Nicolai several years before the war. In his own memoirs, however, the great exponent of cloak-and-dagger, mentions no names, male or female. Chary with his trade secrets, he wrote only in broad generalities and altogether proved himself so close-mouthed and professionally knowledgeable that he subsequently blueprinted the Abwehr, the Gestapo, and other secret bureaus for the Nazis.

In November, 1914, three months after the commencement of the war, Maria married José de Victorica, of Chile, following a whirlwind courtship of four weeks. The vows were exchanged at the Chilean consulate in Hamburg, and the best man, of course, was a member of the Nachrichtendienst.

The span of connubial bliss established some sort of an

ephemeral record. The bridegroom vanished from sight almost at once, lending credence to the supposition that the marriage had been arranged by Nicolai to endow Maria with a neutral citizenship.

She spent the next two years of the war goading on the already hotheaded Sinn Feiners ("Ourselves Alone") in Ireland to greater acts of rebellion against England. One of her instructions was to encourage the young men of this outlawed organization to enlist in the Royal Navy, and then sabotage their ships in various ways, including the placing of small bombs below the waterline and pouring acid into machinery.

Maria was believed to be in Dublin during the bloody Easter rebellion, in 1916, and in June of the same year when Lord Kitchener, Great Britain's Secretary of State for War, was lost aboard HMS *Hampshire*, off the Orkneys, embarking on a secret mission to Russia. Rumors that Maria was involved in a plot to put a dynamiter aboard the ill-fated cruiser, from which only twelve survived, were never proven. The report of the official investigation released after the war, concluded that the ship had struck a mine.

By late autumn of that year, it was increasingly obvious that diplomatic relations with the United States would soon be disrupted completely. Germany's embassy and all of its consulates would be padlocked, as well as perhaps many of its exporting houses and other commercial overseas offices. And then Berlin would be almost deaf and blind to the fast-accelerating developments in Washington.

At best, communications had not been good.

It was time, if it were not already too late, to improve the quality of the Nachrichtendienst's espionage activities in America. Maria, with a veteran agent, Carl Rodiger, using also the alias, Lieutenant Commander Herman Wessels, were to be sent to New York. Their mission was necessarily complex: continue sabotage of ships, also of war factories if possible, keep a watch on North-South America as well as United States-Mexican relationships, and do anything possible to corrode and impede them, report on outbound Allied convoys.

Maria was armed with many letters of introduction, to German firms in New York which would act as her banker, to other contacts, and curiously to the priesthood

The pair entrained from Berlin after New Year's Day, 1917, and sailed from Norway aboard the *Bergensfjord*. The liner called at Kirkwall, Scotland, where the British lost their best opportunity to seize the evanescent Maria. Her existence, under various names, had been known to Allied counterintelligence throughout the war. It was on record that she had operated in Ireland, in Spain, and had on at least one occasion fled homeward through the French lines just before the Deuxième Bureau could pounce.

The passengers of all neutral ships were customarily questioned thoroughly when passing through a port of one of the warring nations, and their belongings were searched. Possibly Maria's Argentinian passport caught the immigration inspectors napping.

Through her porthole, at Kirkwall, Maria also saw for the first time the Grand Fleet in all its majesty at Scapa Flow, the world's mightiest naval anchorage. From here, a short seven months previously, it had steamed furiously out to join in the war's most tremendous and costly naval battle: Jutland.

On January 21, the *Bergensfjord* docked in New York.

Maria registered as Marie de Vussiere at the Knickerbocker Hotel on Times Square and went to work. Two weeks later, on February 4, she drew her first large cash payment, $35,000, from a German exporter with an office on Wall Street, which had received the authorizing cable:

> Give Victorica following message from her lawyers. Lower terms impossible. Will give further instruction earliest and leave nothing untried. Very poor market. Will quote however soonest our terms. Want meanwhile bond. Have already obtained license.

The sender, obviously the Nachrichtendienst, used the curious code signature, "Disconto." The "poor market" in this double talk was indeed the truth. Just the day before, on February 3, diplomatic relations between the United States and Imperial Germany had been severed. The recent sinking of the American steamer *Housatonic* had been but another provocation in the Kaiser's reckless unrestricted submarine warfare.

All naval yards and stations were closed to visitors. The New York militia and naval reserve were called out. The nation was giddily marching headlong toward war through "Preparedness Parades."

"Peace!" cried the former Secretary of State Williams Jennings Bryan.

But it was too late. No one seemed to want peace any more.

Maria recognized her mission was now changing. Instead of a listener and obstructor in a technically neutral nation, she would be reverting to her old role overseas—as spy in a hostile country and, as such, subject to the rules of war.

She moved as "Miss Clark" to the Netherlands Hotel and pondered ways by which she could operate as unobtrusively as possible. Her superiors, however, while equally desirous for her to remain sub rosa, made the fatal mistake of under-estimating their American opposites. They continued to flood messages to Victorica in New York under a false sense of security through which they had wholly deceived themselves.

True, the United States courts had never ordered a spy to be "shot or hung," But the Army in recent months was scoring quiet triumphs in its adolescent but thriving Secret Ink Bureau of MI-8. It was wholly the brainchild of a young, former telegraphist at the Department of State, Herbert O. Yardley.

Through the Civil War and into the Spanish-American War, the United States had relied on codes and ciphers which any smart schoolchild could have broken, given a little time. A Hoosier by birth, Yardley had attracted attention early in his work of deciphering incoming coded cables from America's European embassies and legations and placing them, boldly, on his superior's desk.

By 1917, the now Major Yardley was operating around-the-clock a secret ink laboratory and code room in the War Department. The daily haul of intercepted letters and cables originated not only from sources within the country but from their opposite bureaus in capitals which included London, Paris, Rome, and Tokyo.

The analysts looked for hidden writing while testing many types of reagents as developers. They then sought to translate the banalities, the seemingly innocuous chit-chat about weather, business, trips, sickness.

Illness, for example, usually meant an agent was under surveillance. If "Charlie" had "recovered," he considered the watch to be ended and was back on the job. "Friends" were fellow operatives.

Although the actual skein of tattletale evidence which ultimately led to Maria de Victorica was almost hopelessly complex and ensnarled, the curious circumstances toward its unraveling actually commenced through the carelessness of a paid courier. He happened to be a steward on a Norwegian liner.

Just before he sailed from Christiania, a porter at the Hotel Metropole had given him two messages. One was for a legitimate German contact in New York, the other for a "cover." This "cover" was an elderly widow chosen more or less at random, whose mailbox was ransacked regularly for the expected letters. She was thoroughly ignorant of the use being made of her.

It was accepted practice to try to mail spy messages in countries other than that of true origin. Thus, the postmark became meaningless. In this instance, however, the steward, probably without knowing what he was carrying, became worried about the letters and hid them in his shoes.

By the time the ship docked in New York, the envelopes were so mussed that he determined to address new ones. This he did, and inadvertently switched letters. One of them went to the apartment of a man already under surveillance as a German agent, the other to the cover.

The former letter was grabbed at once by the American agent watching the house of the man under suspicion. It concerned instructions to "take up your business activities" (spying) in South America and to "invest capital in" (make plans for sabotaging) war industries, docks, quicksilver mines, and other worthwhile targets.

Since it was addressed, inside, to the correct name of the cover, the old woman, hitherto unknown to authorities, was located and questioned. She had received some of these mysterious letters herself, she recalled casually, and then thrown them away, since they made no sense at all to her.

The woman, a naturalized citizen of German origin, was in poor financial circumstances. No one could suspect her of spying. She did, however, recall seeing the name "Victorica" in several letters.

Now a cable to British intelligence elicited the information that there was a Victorica, indeed, on the loose. And a copy of the February 4 telegram, authorizing the New York firm to pay her $35,000, was forwarded.

Investigation at that establishment led to other of Victorica's contacts and the finding of actual letters written by her. The important information in almost every case was inscribed in invisible ink. Some of it was so perishable that it would be only partially developed.

Soon fantastic plottings came to light: The marking of "sinking positions" with buoys just off the coast between New York and Cape Hatteras—presumably for the storage of U-boat supplies, including fuel, spare parts, and preserved food—was revealed. The introduction, if possible, of saboteurs on English warships equipped with "lead pencil sticks," or small fire bombs such as used by Von Rintelen, was planned. After April, 1917, with America's belligerency, the orders were extended, necessarily, to include the United States Navy. Blueprints for "operations" against the Panama Canal were sought.

Surely the most imaginative were the orders to a Zurich plasterer for an "altar containing 3 holy figures, 4 columns about 2 meters in height . . . to match 6 meters wide and 3 meters high. Style Renaissance . . . baroque, painting in rural style." Further decodings revealed, as incredible as it seemed, that Victorica and her conspirators had been instructed to import the statuary as a means of bringing high explosives into the country. The hollow figures would be filled with the destructive new chemical. Tetra. None, so far as could be ascertained, had been shipped from Switzerland.

In one letter Victorica made the mistake of asking, "How do you like my specialty, 'Kalium iodatum'?" This was a reagent for bringing out invisible writing. Like Louise de Bettignies and others before her in this profession, the "Baroness" was becoming too sure of herself.

Maria Victorica, however, must have had some notion, if only intuitive, that someone was on her trail. She moved to the Waldorf, then to the Spencer Arms, and finally to a seashore resort hotel, the Nassau, at Long Beach, Long Island. In the latter's baroque sanctuary she could also watch the everswelling outbound convoys.

She had now acquired a secretary, an Irish woman, Margaret Sullivan, who despite of a twenty-five-year residency in the United States had not lost a fierce nationalistic spirit for her homeland.

Meanwhile, greater developments, this spring of 1918, were themselves building toward a climax. Petrograd was a caldron of rioting as the long-seething Russian revolt finally culminated in the Treaty of Brest-Litovsk, taking this huge Czardom out of the war. Rumania and Finland followed with their own separate peace treaties with the Kaiser, who felt compelled to observe: "We are at the decisive moment of the war!"

His generals launched a massive offensive along a fifty-mile British front about twenty miles northeast of Lille. Parisians, at the same time, received a shattering taste of combat as a long-range gun, Big Bertha, started lobbing shells from a fantastic seventy-mile distance.

And in New York, in mid-March, a German woman, who was a younger counterpart of Maria Victorica, was arrested.

Turkish-born Despina Davidovich Storch, twenty-three, claiming to be the divorced wife of a French Army officer, had hobnobbed with East Coast society. Her frequent companion was a Baron de Beville, which inspired her to use the occasional alias "Baroness de Beville."

Apprehended with her was another woman of German extraction, who gave the name Mrs. Elizabeth Charlotte Nix, and two men. All, foolishly enough, claimed French citizenship. Immigration authorities, taking them at their word, recommended they be deported at once. The Department of Justice not only agreed but was happy to do so. There was only suspicion to go on, the faintly incriminating testimony of informers, an intercepted letter or two, the knowledge that the four had gravitated in diplomatic circles before relations were broken. All appeared to have lived far beyond any manifest means of support.

Mme. Storch, for example, registered at the Waldorf. The attractive young blonde too late, however, realized the enormity of her error in professing French citizenship. She was aware of the execution of Mata Hari, for one. On the other hand, she had every reason to know the "softness" of American courts, especially where women were on trial.

Not quite two weeks after her arrest, late on a Saturday night, March 30, as a blustery spring wind whipped across New York harbor, Despina Storch lay back against the pillow of her iron cot in the receiving station, Ellis Island, and bit open a tiny vial of liquid she had carried secretly for a long time. She swallowed the entire contents.

When the matron attempted to rouse her for breakfast, Mme. Storch was dead. The authorities gave their official explanation: pneumonia.

Among the names she had mentioned after her arrest was

that of Maria de Victorica. The latter's longevity as a useful spy had been remarkable—virtually the war long, and on two fronts, in Europe and the United States.

A young girl, who carried both money and messages to Victorica this same fateful spring, was the last link that closed the chain drawing around the German agent. She herself had been observed in her visits to the houses of two other suspects whose guilt or innocence had not yet been established. One April afternoon, it was decided to follow her.

The trail led first, of all places, to St. Patrick's Cathedral, on Fifth Avenue. The girl knelt briefly in prayer, then departed. Left behind only momentarily in the pew was a folded newspaper which another "worshipper," a man, quickly picked up. Then he, too, hurried out of the cathedral.

He hailed a taxi, which took him to Pennsylvania Station, where he caught a train for Long Beach. At the Nassau Hotel, he sat for a moment in the lobby; then, as the girl had done little more than an hour ago at St. Patrick's, he left his newspaper and walked casually from the hotel.

In a moment, a plumpish blonde woman appeared, carrying papers and magazines of her own. She sat, seemingly absorbed in their contents. Then, forgetting her own but gathering the one the man had discarded, she strode toward the elevator.

Inside the newspaper? Twenty thousand dollars in bank notes smuggled across the Mexican border from the German embassy in that neutral country.

Maria Victorica was arrested a week later, on April 27. For two days she led American agents on fruitless missions here and there, to Washington Heights, back to Long Island, to lower Manhattan until finally they realized she was merely stalling for time.

Why had she come to the United States?

"I really cannot say, unless it was because I wanted to marry again," she explained glibly. She added that the tens of thousands of dollars she had spent were merely for "living expenses and my maid."

In her room, searchers found an unusual bit of evidence: a silk scarf impregnated with German "F" secret ink.

Together with Wessels (alias Rodiger, Schmidt, Brown, and some other pseudonyms), Mme. Victorica was indicted on charges of conspiracy to commit espionage in time of war. A treason indictment against five lesser American co-defendants was more lengthy:

"The conspirators gave aid and comfort to the German government and to Rodiger and Victorica by furnishing for the use of the said Rodiger and said Victorica such addresses as they would from time to time determine, at which communications from the Imperial German Government might be received by mail, for the purpose of concealing the said communications and the fact of such communicating from the officers and officials of the United States. In and by assisting the said Rodiger and Victorica in securing chemicals and other ingredients for the manufacture of bombs with the intention that said bombs would be placed on docks and piers in the United States and on ships sailing from ports of the United States for the purpose of causing injury and destruction of docks, piers, and ships which docks, piers, and ships would be used to transport troops and military supplies of the United States.

"By assisting the said Rodiger and the said Victorica to procure persons of Irish descent in the United States (who

would be willing and could be so induced) to secure employment as workmen and sailors on the aforesaid docks,
piers, and ships for the purpose of planting the aforesaid
bombs thereon, and in and by assisting the said Rodiger and
the said Victorica in causing injury to and the destruction of
quicksilver mines in the United States by such means as the
said citizen conspirators, the said Rodiger and the said Victorica, might devise for the purpose of thereby diminishing
and stopping the supply of quicksilver used in the production of munitions of war for the United States, and in and by
such other acts which the said conspirators had not determined upon but which they would determine from time to
time would be best adapted to encourage, aid, assist, and
comfort said Rodiger and the said Victorica in performing
the duties with which they were charged by the Imperial
German Government in its war against the United States."

When, in Federal district court in New York sections of
the Espionage Act were read providing that those convicted
"shall be punished by death or . . . ," Victorica quickly
pressed what reporters described as a "jeweled hand" to her
face, then drew it away. She apparently had not listened to
the somewhat milder alternative "or by imprisonment for
not more than thirty years."

The Justice Department had squandered its time. Two of
the defendants were "in absentia," seeking refuge in Mexico
or Ireland, or even in the mazes of New York itself. One of
them brought to trial later was freed after the jury could not
possibly come to a decision.

By the time the court was ready to hear the cases against
the others the war was over. And millions of disillusioned
Americans acted like debauchers on the morning after.

What was it all about, they asked? What were we fighting
for?

It was different, naturally, in Europe. But in the United States, it was as though, now, the people were mad only at themselves for this "great adventure" they had so excitedly sought. It was the end not so much of a quick nightmare but of a sustained period of hallucinations.

No longer did there appear such acute differentiation between the "good guys" and the "bad guys." The jail doors for the latter, if bad they truly were, were quietly opened, one by one. It was not such a stigma any more to possess a German name. Even boardinghouse keepers of German extraction could go about their business in Hoboken, Milwaukee, St. Louis, and elsewhere without worrying about sudden sharp knockings on the front door. And it was safe to fish, to walk near bridges or factories, without the lurking fear of being hauled off to jail at any instant.

Victorica spent the final months of the war alternately at Bellevue Hospital and in an army base on Staten Island. Her health, from not wholly revealed causes, was failing. Some reports indicated that she was giving full testimony on her fellow conspirators in America and on the intricate workings of the Nachrichten Bureau. An equal number of rumors held that Victorica would not cooperate with her captors.

In either case, one lurid theory had it, she was secretly taking poison, little by little, or narcotics in order to kill herself and thus escape what she fancied would be the ultimate wrath of Colonel Nicolai for failing in her mission. In fact a team of doctors from Johns Hopkins Hospital in Baltimore supposedly was hurried to Staten Island one evening to save her life after an overdose of barbituates.

It was rumored simultaneously that her husband had been seized in France and possibly shot. However, since Maria had not seen José since shortly after their marriage, it was reasonable to assume that her grief, if his death *were* true, would be something short of profound.

She was released under $5,000 bond after the Armistice in the care of Catholic sisters. She lived in their convent for nearly two years, devoting her time to prayer and contemplation. It was believed that she attempted to return to Germany, but either could not or did not wish to post the additional bond required by the Justice Department, since she was still under federal indictment.

In the summer of 1920, stricken with pneumonia, she was removed to a private sanatorium, known as Dr. Maluk's, on East 78th Street. The infection was fatal. She died on August 12, 1920. Requiem mass was solemnized at St. Vincent Ferrer's Church on Lexington Avenue, and her remains interred at the Gate of Heaven Cemetery, Hawthorne, Westchester County.

Still recorded in the name of her long-deceased attorney, the tomb is forgotten and meaningless to most who come to mourn at other resting sites. It is simply "Grave 8, Plot B" in the cemetery superintendent's office—a very anticlimactic ending indeed for the most colorful spy to operate in the United States during the first World War.

Part 2

••>

WOMEN SPIES COME OF AGE

5

DOLLS IN MUFTI

••> *Velvalee Dickinson, 1944*

"Dear Friend," the long, rambling letter to Señor Inez Lopez de Molinali, in Buenos Aires, commenced, "you probably wonder what has become of me as I haven't written to you for so long. We have had a pretty bad month or so. . . ."

And so began one of the most curious spy cases to come out of World War II, or quite likely any conflict. It was one in which money, glory, flamboyance, the thrill of the hunt and being hunted apparently played no part at all. Possibly its inspiration was a blind passion for a country other than one's own. If not, then Velvalee Dickinson's betrayal was totally without impetus. And that was most improbable, too.

Velvalee Malvena Blucher was the smallest girl among her immediate playmates in Sacramento, barely five feet tall. Sparrowlike, straw blonde, and wholly nondescript in appearance, Velvalee was the daughter of plain but well-to-do parents, Otto Blucher, West Virginia-born, and the former Elizabeth C. Bottoms, from Kentucky.

At the age of eighteen, in June, 1911, Velvalee graduated from Sacramento High School, and from a private seminary in Berkeley two years later. Her education was continued at Sacramento Junior College and, finally, at Leland Stanford University. She qualified for her Bachelor of Arts in 1917, after a year's attendance. For some unstated reason, the degree was not formally awarded until 1937.

Like all spies of consequence, Velvalee's personal biography is less than definitive. Apparently she did not work full time until 1925 when she was employed by the file department of a San Francisco bank. Two years later she became a bookkeeper with a brokerage house in the same city. It was a firm which handled many Japanese accounts, especially in produce brokerage.

There she met Lee Taylor Dickinson, its owner. Her subsequent marriage to him was said to be her third, after two unsuccessful tries. If so, it is not on record who were her first two mates.

Soon, Velvalee gained the reputation of being an excellent businesswoman. As a somewhat dubious bonus, her unusual interest in her clients caused her to be tagged by neighbors as a "Jap-lover."

In the early 1930's, Lee Dickinson extended his business to the Imperial Valley, where many Japanese farmers had settled. Velvalee's name, not surprisingly, became well known to Japanese consular and military attachés on the West Coast. The Dickinsons—possibly at first for business reasons—joined the Japanese-American Society, and were conscientious attendants at activities which in any way were connected with the Japanese colony.

The Dickinsons were so popular in fact that when Velvalee was dropped from the Society for nonpayment of dues, a confidential attaché at the Japanese consulate in San Francisco, Kaoru Nakashima, gallantly anted up for her. Velvalee was reinstated.

This possibly exaggerated identification with his customers did not save Dickinson's brokerage firm from failing in 1935. Perhaps it even accelerated the process.

Velvalee sought and obtained various jobs: with the California State Emergency Relief Administration, in San Francisco, and with the County Welfare Department as a social service investigator.

Nothing any more seemed to win the Dickinsons a livelihood. Conceivably the ever mounting sentiment against the Japanese community, the Niseis, made it difficult for Lee to work with his business and professional counterparts.

"Jap-lover!" already carried an increasing stigma.

In 1937, in despair, the couple moved to New York City, taking up residence in a small hotel, on West 11th Street, near Washington Square. On the last day of the year, Velvalee accepted a position as doll saleswoman at Bloomingdale's Department Store at eighteen dollars a week.

She had always been fond of dolls and their dresses as a hobby. Now, she turned this interest into breadwinning channels. She was a sellout success, so much so that she soon opened her own shop in her new apartment, at 680 Madison Avenue. She was, she confided, "tired of accepting orders from others."

Business was so good that she moved to a spacious street frontage store at 718 Madison. Meteorically she had become an authority on antique, rare, exquisitely fashioned and clothed dolls, with a price tag starting at a minimum of twenty-five and soaring into the hundreds of dollars.

Velvalee Dickinson attracted a nationwide clientele, including movie and Broadway stars, assorted social celebrities, and affluent men and women of the carriage trade.

Curiously, however, in spite of outward indications of success, Velvalee was constantly borrowing relatively small sums of money from her friends and business associates. It must have been at least mildly perplexing to them, none of whom, however, had it in his or her heart to refuse.

Among her friends was Kaname Wakasugi, the Japanese consul general, and Ichira Yokoyama, the naval attaché at the embassy in Washington. She was elected to membership in the Japanese Institute of New York and was a frequent caller at the Nippon Club. Very often she dressed in traditional Japanese attire, including headgear and footwear. Certainly her diminutive stature added to her affinity with these Asiatics. As a grown woman, she still weighed not quite a hundred pounds.

It seemed improbable, however, that Consul Wakasugi, Attaché Yokoyama, or the other Orientals with whom she sipped diluted sake or stronger tea at the Nippon Club were interested in rare dolls—certainly not the kind that were made of wax or plaster and were displayed at the Madison Avenue store.

After December 7, 1941, her circle of friends was automatically shrunken in numbers. The diplomatic staffs were sent home on neutral ships; other Japanese aliens were interned for the duration or subsequently exchanged for American citizens caught in Japan. Many known sympathizers were placed under surveillance.

Velvalee remained on the move for a least the first half of 1942. With her husband, she traveled first to Seattle, then to San Francisco, and back to New York in March. She re-opened her store for several days, then returned to Seattle, with a call at Portland.

The Dickinsons then journeyed south to Oakland, California, and after a pause there traveled through the southern part of the United States before returning to New York. The pair possessed a seemingly inordinate amount of hundred-dollar bills for paying an employee or repaying debts; they also changed them in adjacent stores.

It was not on vacation to see old friends that Velvalee had been traveling this first year of America's involvement in the war. Transportation was no simple matter those days, with priorities, crowds thronging the waiting rooms in whistle stop and large city railroad station alike, troop trains getting the green light on all lines, servicemen on furlough commandeering what little space was available on regular passenger trains. The automobile was virtually out of the question because of gasoline rationing.

And as she and her husband kept on the go, peculiar letters, one by one, began to arrive in the Federal Bureau of Investigation. Each had been addressed to a Señora Inez Lopez de Molinali, 2563 O'Higgins Street, Buenos Aires, Argentina. And each had been sent back to the return address on the envelope because no such person as Señora de Molinali could be found at the O'Higgins Street number given.

Mary Wallace, of East High Street, Springfield, Ohio, was thoroughly baffled as she read and reread the letter to "Dear Friend," which was signed in a reasonably faithful copy of her own handwriting.

. . . We have had a pretty bad month or so. My little nephew the one I adore so has malignant tumor on the brain and isn't expected to live so we are all so crushed we do not know what we are doing. They are giving him X-ray on the head and they hope to check it but give us absolutely no hope in a complete cure and maybe not even any relief. I am completely crushed.

You asked me to tell you about my collection. A month ago I had to give a talk to an Art Club so I talked about my dolls and figurines. The only new dolls I have are three lovely Irish dolls. One of these dolls is an old fisherman with a net over his back, another is an old woman with wood on her back and the third is a little boy.

Everyone seemed to enjoy my talk I can only think of our sick boy these days.

You wrote me that you had sent a letter to Mr. Shaw. Well I went to see Mr. Shaw. He destroyed your letter, you know he has been ill. His car was damaged but is being repaired now. I saw a few of his family about. They all say Mr. Shaw will be back to work soon.

I do hope my letter is not too sad. There is not much I can write you about these days.

I came on this short trip for mother for business, before I try to make out her income report. That is also why I am learning to type. Everyone seems busy these days. The streets are full of people.

Remember me to your family. Sorry I haven't written to you for so long.

Truly,

Mary Wallace

P.S. Mother wanted to go to Louisville but due to our worry the Louisville plan was put out of our minds now.

Between February, when Mary Wallace received her letter, and August, 1942, letters—all rambling on about dolls— were received by equally incredulous women in Portland,

Oregon (two letters); Spokane, Washington; and Colorado Springs, Colorado.

As in the case of Mary Wallace, their own signatures were approximated, and a certain intimacy with their personal lives was apparent. It was true, each of the ladies admitted to FBI investigators, they had some interest in rare dolls, but *who* was Señora Inez de Molinali in Buenos Aires? None had ever heard of her.

But each woman had either called upon Velvalee Dickinson at her shop, had corresponded with her, or had been visited by her. And as a matter of fact, at least two of the four recalled differences with the doll expert over prices or something pertaining to their order.

Velvalee's spite had, in part, inspired her use of the women's names. Her spitefulness was to be her undoing.

Soon, there was no doubt that all letters had been written on the same typewriter, by the same person. The code was "open" and very obvious. Mary Wallace's letter referred to the destroyer *Shaw* which had been damaged at Pearl Harbor and was in the Puget Sound Navy Yard undergoing repairs at the time the letter was written.

"New dolls" alluded to new warships about to operate in the Pacific, including the "fisherman with a net," meaning an aircraft carrier with antitorpedo nets, escorted by "an old woman with wood on her back" (an old battleship with temporary or renovated superstructure), and "a little boy," a destroyer.

The postscript was absurdly transparent—the cruiser *Louisville* was at sea, and Velvalee could not obtain infomation requested about her.

Mary Wallace did have a nephew who was ill, with a mortal brain ailment, and had talked before an art club. She also had been in the doll shop at 718 Madison Avenue. She would later express amazement that she did not make any association of these facts when first she opened the mysterious letter.

Ship movements and repairs, thinly veiled by Velvalee's references to broken dolls, doll hospitals (shipyards), and the dispatching of dolls to various destinations, dominated the correspondence. The interpretations to be attached to English, French, or Dutch dolls, accompanied by reference to a geographical location, were obvious.

Especially imaginative was her mention of a "German bisque doll" dressed in a "hula skirt," to be sent to a doll hospital in Seattle. This referred to a warship damaged at Honolulu, although "German bisque" was employed only to confuse.

Yet more specific was the reference to seven small dolls in another of the letters, which the writer said she would attempt to make look as if they were "seven real Chinese dolls," comprising a family of father, grandmother, grandfather, mother and three children.

This letter, mailed from Oakland, assumed a timeliness when it was ascertained that seven warships steamed through the golden Gate just prior to the time the letter was written and mailed. Details about damage they had sustained might have been helpful to the enemy had Velvalee been able to convey what she apparently intended in this unique but crude attempt at slipping items of military intelligence through the censor.

Everything the five recipients said pointed to Velvalee Dickinson. Yet, the FBI waited.

Events which had nothing to do with her own feelings or the actions of counteragents shaped the course of Velvalee's life after 1942. Stricken with a heart attack after their rather frantic travels to the West Coast, Lee Dickinson died in March, 1943.

His widow, while maintaining her doll shop, considered moving back to the West Coast, where she offered $15,000 as part interest in a hotel. This sum was approximately twice the amount of the life insurance left by her husband.

At Christmas, Bloomingdale's, searching around for an attractive window display, remembered their erstwhile doll saleswoman. The department store's promotion department was grateful when Velvalee agreed to loan several dozen of her dolls for the purpose.

It was Velvalee's last favorable publicity. On January 21, 1944, FBI men, certain of their case, arrested her in the safety deposit vaults of a bank one block south of the doll shop.

She was taken completely by surprise. This was strange, since recently customers she had never seen before, both men and women, wandered in to ask questions which betrayed an ignorance about antique and national dolls.

"Bitterly," by the description of the men who had come to arrest her, Velvalee fought them off. Dressed in a simple brown overcoat and wearing a plain blue hat, this birdlike, graying little woman presented a preposterous spectacle as she bit, clawed, kicked, and smashed with pocketbook at the government agents.

When they finally handcuffed her, they found $15,940 in cash in her deposit box, of which $10,000 was in $100 Federal Reserve notes. Many of them later were traced to the Yokohama Specie Bank in New York and to the Japanese consulate previous to the Pearl Harbor attack.

Quieter, but still distraught during her arraignment at the

United States Court House, in lower Manhattan, Velvalee
contributed to the lexicon of excuse-making when asked why
she had not placed some of her funds in U.S. War Bonds.

"I did not know how to buy them," she declared.

Velvalee could not raise a $25,000 bond. She remained in
jail pending her trial—on dual charges of espionage and of
violating the censorship laws. On the former, she faced the
death penalty; and if convicted. as the more sensational
among newspapers luridly speculated, she might have become the first woman to be executed in the United States as
a spy.

Her request to bring her collection of Japanese musical
recordings and a small record player with her into the
Women's House of Detention was refused. And so, as the
fateful spring of 1944 moved on, Velvalee sat quietly in
prison and waited.

While Velvalee could well ponder her future—if indeed
there would be any—three other women received prison
sentences on espionage charges in Federal District Court,
Detroit. They were Grace Buchanan-Dineen, thirty-four-
year-old Canadian-born brunette who sometimes called herself "Countess"; Mrs. Theresa Behrens, forty-four, a naturalized citizen; and Mrs. Emma Elise Leonhardt.

Judge Edward J. Moinet asserted that Mrs. Behrens, originally from Yugoslavia, was "the heart and soul of the espionage conspiracy in Detroit . . . the record shows that
overt acts were committed to this end . . . information as to
our defense plants or troop or ship movements."

Mrs. Behrens, who had argued stridently with the jurist,
fainted when she heard her sentence: twenty years, eight
more years than meted the "Countess," fifteen more than
Mrs. Leonhardt.

"Countess" Buchanan-Dineen, however, was the most colorful of the trio. Shortly before the war a Vassar exchange student in Budapest had contacted her and persuaded her to attend a Nazi foreign espionage school.

She arrived in the United States via clipper in October, 1941, with a notebook containing names of contacts and a rather fuzzy mission to send back production information on American heavy industry.

Her manner and her good looks were easy introduction to American society. Popular and acceptable, she seemed to cultivate, especially, those affiliated with the Ford Motor Company and the Pullman Standard Car Manufacturing Company.

Sometimes, she was "Miss Smith." But "Miss Smith" or "Countess," Grace Buchanan-Dineen was not very successful as a secret agent. The FBI picked up her trail before year's end, and although she was unaware of it, counteragents were funneling spurious production figures, including those of the giant Willow Run bomber plant, to her to transmit back to Germany.

When finally confronted, the "Countess" confessed her role and agreed to continue cooperating, pending her indictment and trial.

None of the "Detroit group" appeared to possess the imagination of Velvalee Dickinson, whose brother, Oswald Blucher, in the meanwhile was located and arrested. His loyalty in refusing to discuss his sister in any way resulted in a ten-day jail sentence for contempt of court. He was in no way accused of being involved in her exploits.

As her trial date neared, it became increasingly obvious that Velvalee had been living far beyond her mediocre means. Internal Revenue files revealed that Velvalee Dickinson's total income reported in 1939 was $2,616.20. In 1942 she claimed a loss of $1,135.67.

Her arraignment came on July 6, the day of the invasion of Normandy. All mention of it was submerged in the overwhelming news of that day. Her two court-appointed attorneys asked that her trial be delayed until national excitement and passions cooled.

Federal Court Judge Stephen S. Chandler granted the postponement until July 28, while at the same time dismissing the espionage charge as "highly circumstantial." Velvalee had already pleaded innocent to it.

On the twenty-eighth, a quiet, black-gloved, black-dressed Mrs. Dickinson arrived, almost cringing, in the corridors of the Federal Court House. This was in striking contrast to the defiant, bantam fighter arrested in the bank vault.

"Who are all these people?" she asked, looking at the special agents, reporters, spectators, and clerks in the courtroom.

As Velvalee twisted her handkerchief in her hands one of her lawyers, Maurice Shaine, pleaded for clemency, stressing his client's claim that her husband was entirely to blame.

"She is," asserted United States Attorney James B. McNally, "a woman who sold her country to the Japs for money. What she did was unspeakably foul . . . borders on treason!"

Then, with whimsical irony, he noted that she had finally been betrayed by her own dolls, dolls which in effect had "talked." She was, as well, betrayed by her beloved Japanese, who had switched agents in Buenos Aires without telling her. Was this by chance?

The trial was of short duration. The lawyers, both prosecuting and defending, agreed on a "guilty" plea to the censorship violation charge. Leniency was sought.

On August 14, Judge Shackelford Miller, Jr., sterner than Judge Chandler, sentenced Velvalee to the maximum of ten years in prison and a $10,000 fine.

"It is hard to believe," he declared, "that some people do not realize that our nation is engaged in a life-and-death struggle. Any help given to the enemy means the death of American boys who are fighting for our national security.

"You, as a natural-born citizen having a university education, and selling out to the Japanese, were certainly engaged in espionage. I think that you have been given every consideration by the government. The indictment to which you have pleaded guilty is a serious matter. . . ."

Only then, after she left the court, did Velvalee admit to FBI agents that it was she who typed the five incriminating doll letters, using correspondence from her customers for forging their signatures. Information about the ships she said she had obtained through questioning residents living near West Coast shipyards and naval stations. She continued in her efforts to attribute culpability to her husband.

She went so far as to insist that, immediately after his death, while his body was still in bed, she searched the room and found "a big wad of cash and a code book" under the mattress cover. There was no substantiation for this ghoulish assertion.

She now, belatedly, admitted the nature of the doll-warship code, which cryptanalysts had already ascertained for themselves.

Velvalee entrained for the Reformatory for Women, in Alderson, West Virginia—and oblivion. On April 23, 1951, she was mandatorily paroled, returning to her long-ago address on West 11th Street, in New York. She reported to the United States Probation Officer, Southern District of New York, until February 13, 1954, at which time, by statute, the specialist in rare and antique dolls became no longer of any legal or criminal interest to the United States of America.

Her apartment house has changed character twice since that time, as women's dormitories for two New York institutions of higher learning. The list of former tenants is lost. The trail of this most unusual spy in America has seemingly grown cold.

But perhaps, just perhaps, the answer is to be found in an obscure Japanese tearoom in the same Washington Square neighborhood where a bent, white-haired, sparrowlike old woman, sometimes wearing Japanese prints (discreetly beneath her overcoat), comes in to sip from fragile dainty cups —and think conceivably long, long thoughts about what might have been if she had not been so spiteful.

6

⋮

NEVER SO FEW

⋯➤ *Britain's Heroines of World War II*

They were present-day St. Joans of Arc, martyrs and potential martyrs to a cause and principles new perhaps only because of twentieth-century terminology. These ladies and
young girls owed allegiance to Great Britain, the Allies, and
their personal ideals as they fought a lonely, unyielding war
against the Nazis. When they lost, their fate, too often, was
scarcely equaled in the dark annals of history.

It was difficult enough then to believe that it could ever
have happened. Nearly a quarter of a century afterward it is
no less incomprehensible.

They were slipped clandestinely into France for sabotage,
espionage, communications, and liaison between the underground and the Allied fighting forces in uniform. Most of
their operations were coordinated and endowed with a surprising amount of formality by a war-born, unusually effective agency; it bore the oblique title: Special Operations
Executive.

Wholly unknown to the vast majority of Britons until after

the war, "SOE"—as it was inevitably referred to by its dedicated personnel—still awaits a fully lucid historian. To those who served in it and died for it, however, SOE was as real and palpable as, say, the Republican party or the Baptist Church.

Male and female without distinction, they went off to France, usually parachuting at night, to work in all areas of occupied France and the Lowlands in small, tightly knit units, whose very code designations bespoke the imaginative quality of their "org."

There was Donkeyman and Monkeypuzzle, Helmsman and Pimiento, Clergyman, Saint, and Stockbroker, Woodcutter and Juggler, Ventriloquist and Greenheart, among others.

These "circuits," as they were labeled at London headquarters—appropriately enough in an unpretentious house in Baker Street, where Conan Doyle long before had located Sherlock Holmes—were composed of men and women whose ages, interests, and professional or lack of professional background were as diverse and mixed as their individual assignments. Many of the female operatives were exquisitely attractive. In other times, they could have enjoyed brilliant careers on the stage. One of them had in fact been an acclaimed Polish beauty queen.

However, pulchritude was not one of the prerequisites for employment by SOE. One of the first to arrive was a somewhat nondescript forty-eight-year-old grandmother whose previous experience had encompassed nothing more unusual or hazardous than hotel receptionist. Yvonne Rudellat ("Jacqueline") was rowed through the surf one stormy night in July, 1942, from an offshore corvette, onto the coast of southern France.

This aggressive member of "Physician" helped blow up a

power station and two locomotives before being captured by the Gestapo. And even then, Grandmother Rudellat fought it out until her last revolver bullet was spent.

The numbers of women agents in the "org" was not itself consequential—no more than fifty. Their deeds were. Their bravery was wholly worthy of that manifested by Yvonne Rudellat (who died of illness at Belsen concentration camp in April, 1945).

Churchill could have extended his tribute to the RAF's valor during the Battle of Britain to applaud these other few to whom so many owed so much. They fought and died in the most dangerous, uncompromising war of all, wholly unprotected by the old Hague Convention which had sought at the turn of the century to "civilize" warfare. It proved a forlorn hope.

These women could expect no quarter. They were denied even the objective, elementary consideration which is the due of a prisoner of war.

From the group sacrifice of SOE's ladies there emerges inevitably not one but many immortals, women we cannot readily forget—in effect, a composite heroine. It is not possible here to do justice to all. These are the accounts of but a few:

An embarkation officer at a secondary airfield in the Midlands could scarcely fail to notice his darkly beautiful passenger.

"In a group of heavily armed and equipped men," he would recall, "waiting to take off from the same airfield, Violette was slim, debonair. She wore a flowered frock, white sandals, and earrings which she had bought in Paris during her first mission. She zipped up her flying suit, adjusted her parachute, shook her hair loose and climbed into the aircraft."

Violette Szabo was riding this single-engined Lysander toward a date with destiny. At twenty-two, the young mother had lived the equivalent of several average lifetimes. She was no average woman, however—a "fiery character," among other attributes, as her superiors admiringly thought of her.

This June 7, the day after the Normandy invasion, Violette was joining the "Salesman" circuit, bound for Salon La Tour, two hundred miles south of Paris. Like thousands of paratroopers already plummeting out of the skies over the Channel coast, Violette, or "Louise," would be descending into the verdant Limoges country of France.

Violette's sister agents joined for reasons of their own. She herself could point to an obvious and valid one, just as Sarah Thompson generations before her. Her husband had been killed fighting Rommel in North Africa.

Violette was the product of a World War I romance. Her father, Charles Bushell, had returned shortly after the Armistice to marry the French girl he had met and loved in Picardy. Although Violette was born in Paris, in 1921, during a period when Bushell was operating a taxi for tourists, she grew up in the southwest Brixton section of London. She was known from childhood as a tomboy, although a lithe and noticeably pretty one.

Rather short, but muscular, Violette could swim, run, do handstands and the range of difficult gymnastics, competing on the same basis with older boys. She became a Dead-eye Dick at London's midway of shooting galleries as well as those at the nearby seaside resort, Brighton.

In her later teens, this English Annie Oakley used to boast, "I never paid for my cigarettes." She won them all by knocking clay ducks and pigeons off the back stops.

After the fall of France in the spring of 1940, Violette met a Free French soldier, Etienne Szabo. Their courtship lasted but a few weeks before Charles Bushell was shaking hands with his son-in-law and wishing him well.

A daughter, Tania, was born two years later, a few months before her father lost his life, in October, 1942. Her mother, who had been working in an aircraft factory, then joined the FANY's, the First Aid Nursing Yeomanry of a historic British organization, the Women's Transport Service.

Since this did not satisfy Violette's desire for the front lines, she arranged an interview with the SOE. Offered one of the approximately three thousand administrative jobs, she declined, and was then assigned to secret agent training. Allied agents, given their preliminary as well as postgraduate training in espionage and sabotage in England, had been moving in and out of France for several years, almost reminiscent in some respects of the tourist traffic of past days. They were augmenting and, especially, directing the accumulating thousands of resistance fighters already committed in a struggle to the death.

Violette threw herself into the training with a zest which might have been expected of the onetime girl athlete. Her natural skill and fast reflexes, however, still were not positive insurance against accidents. She sprained an ankle during a hard parachute landing late in 1943.

She was not ready for her first assignment until April, 1944. This would be a short inspection, accompanied by a war-wise, veteran agent, Philip Liewer, into the Rouen-Channel coast region to reconnoiter for the coming D-Day invasion, and also to check on agents whose radios had grown disturbingly silent.

The pair did not locate other SOE members, although

Liewer found a "wanted" poster of himself on a wall, offering a sizable reward. He tore it off, folded and pocketed it.

There was no doubt that the city of Rouen and the lushly green countryside were both alert to some vast military operation in the making. Violette and her escort reported "inquisitive" Nazis everywhere, not so much in the routine counterspy business but endeavoring to resolve the dual questions: *when* and *where?*

The two spent three weeks in this highly "sensitive" area, with a brief visit to Paris, then were picked up by a Lysander and flown home.

These return flights, made possible through the daring and finesse of pilots, were becoming so successful—from unlit cow pastures and brussels sprouts fields—that soon DC-3's and other twin-engined aircraft were also used. Some of them were armed.

Out of more than one hundred such homeward journeys, only two planes were lost. A third, damaged in landing, was hidden under hay and other camouflage, repaired by the Maquis with parts dropped the next night, then flown home with its passengers, only two days behind schedule.

There were informal "London airports" all over France. The Gestapo was constantly frustrated, since tire prints and the telltale skid mark, whether on tall, thick grass or in soft earth which might have been found overnight, never appeared again in the same field.

During the next two months Violette's work, with the "Salesman" circuit, was interrupted twice by arrests and questioning. Her perfect French and play-acting ability secured her speedy release each time. But her luck was running out.

Late in August, Violette, accompanied by a French agent,

"Anastasie" (Jacques Dufour), with an especially high price on his head, was surrounded in a small house in the environs of Salon La Tour. Determined to bag both quarries, the Gestapo, augmented by SS Trüppen, Hitler's elite guard, had brought up two armored cars.

The athletic Violette, the crack shot of the shilling shooting galleries, seemed to know it was all over this time. Wounded in the arm during the initial exchange of shots, she managed to persuade Anastasie to escape, while she covered him with his rapid-firing Sten gun. He not only succeeded but lived to tell of his female colleague's bravery.

She remained in motion, sending bursts at her besiegers, first from one window, then another. The armored cars sprayed the building with heavy-caliber machine-gun bullets, riddling the walls with holes. The rooms filled with clouds of pulverized plaster.

Violette observed first one, then another of the Nazis fall. She could not be sure how many she had killed or wounded.

The uneven battle could not long continue. Her ammunition finally was exhausted. And so was "Louise." She was taken prisoner by an apparently admiring SS (*Schütz-Staffel* or "shooting stick") Oberst who offered her a cigarette. He quickly withdrew it as she spat in his face and shouted: "Swine!"

Violette was marched onto a train, under exceptionally heavy guard, for Paris. For several days she was interrogated, to no avail, at Fresnes prison, a way-stop for women suspects on the journey of doubtful return to far worse places of confinement in Germany. Female agents and resistance workers of all nationalities in the Allied forces were questioned and sometimes tortured inside these grim walls.

In early September, she was started eastward on a train

containing almost forty agents. Among them was the flamboyant, imaginative Wing Commander Forest Frederick Yeo-Thomas. Known as the "White Rabbit," he had escaped time and again from a series of "impregnable" prison fortresses including Colditz.

Violette distinguished herself during an air raid when the train was halted. She moved around the cars, from which all guards had fled to refuge, distributing water to prisoners. She urged those who sought to take advantage of an obvious opportunity for flight to stay where they were until at least they could ascertain their chances of success.

She survived several German prisons during the fall, winter, and spring. She was tortured "atrociously," by official British pronouncement, although there exists some evidence to the contrary.

Finally, in April, 1945, she was led out of her cell at the huge, infamous Ravensbruck women's concentration camp, forty miles north of Berlin. With her were two "couriers," about whom little is known, Denise Bloch ("Ambroise") and Lillian Rolfe ("Nadine"). With the war's end only days away, the three were shot, in quick succession, in the nape of the neck.

Brixton and Brighton had lost a lovely little "tomboy" and riflewoman.

This sentence, resulting from no trial, was, as with others before it, partly the product of towering Nazi frustration at her consistent refusal to collaborate or to drop even the most meager hints of SOE activities or membership. It was also, in part, the manifestation of increasingly psychotic rage over the obvious reality that the Third Reich—which the Fuehrer had promised would endure a thousand years—was crumbling like Pompeii under the fury of a Vesuvius.

Violette Bushell Szabo's posthumous George Cross, Britain's highest civilian honor (ranking with the Victoria Cross), and her Croix de Guerre proved pathetic playthings which really did not go very far to make up to little Tania for the loss of "Mummy."

Violette was a personality acutely her own, even as no two SOE agents were alike, except for a common denominator of unusual courage and compulsion to serve. "Madeleine," or "Jeanne Marie," her other code name, was as attractive as Violette, but totally different in lineage and character. Noor Inayat Khan (the "Khan" meaning only her ladylike heritage in a curious, archaic caste system) was tall and dark. Her father, an Indian musician and mystic, married an American girl (a distant cousin of Mary Baker Eddy, founder of the Church of Christ, Scientist) during a New York visit.

Noor was born on New Year's Day, 1914, within the Kremlin. Her father's friendship with Leo Tolstoy had something to do with this unusual birthplace. However, the child grew up in France, where her schooling was extensive.

Musical, literary, she had inherited much of her father's feeling of the supernatural and belief in personal prophecy. She lived a sort of continuing apocalypse, this latter generation Indian princess who had been aptly described as "radiating grace."

Closer emotionally to her father possibly than even she could realize, Noor suffered irreparable loss at his sudden death, when she was fifteen. Writing children's stories— ultimately for Radio Paris—assuaged in some measure her grief. In fact, she might have made a career of this form of literature had not a war changed many persons' plans.

She fled with her brother to England when the Germans invaded France in the spring of 1940, settling in Oxford.

When her brother joined the Royal Navy, Noor enlisted in the Women's Auxiliary Air Force as an Aircraftsman 3C.

Her proficiency as a radio operator led to her transfer to SOE in February, 1943. There was no question as to her courage or loyalty. There *was* as to her stability for the job.

"A vague, dreamy creature," was the opinion of a colleague. "Too emotional and sensitive," pronounced one of her instructors. While yet a third teacher suggested her dazzling beauty and charm tended to obscure the fact that she was not "overburdened with brains."

These harsh opinions were overruled, if only because of an insatiable demand for wireless experts in the underground.

On June 16, 1943, Noor was landed near Paris with two others: Mrs. Cecily Lefort, forty-four-year-old Irish-born Continental yachtswoman; and Diana Rowden, twenty-nine, who was herself well known in sailing circles. Most recently she had handled the tiller of a yacht with the singularly prophetic name, *Sans Peur*.

Noor joined the veteran team of the handsome Francis Suttill ("Prosper," from whose code designation the group took its name), Gilbert Norman ("Archambaud"), also a wireless operator, and dark-eyed, beautiful Andrée Borrel ("Denise"), one of the first women parachuted into France, who had aided in the escape of several hundred downed Allied airmen.

A twenty-three-year-old former French nurse, Andrée was "a perfect lieutenant, an excellent organizer who shares all dangers." She had to her credit the bonus of wrecking a power station.

"Prosper" operated at the Ecole Nationale d'Agriculture in the suburb of Grignon, near Versailles. Noor was not bent over her transmitter long, however, before the Gestapo smashed "Prosper" to pieces. She was the only member to elude arrest.

Now, the local *Stürmbahnführer*, Joseph Kieffer, made a curious pact with his three captives. He bargained their lives against their revealing caches of weapons dropped for the underground. He would honor his part so long as the trio remained physically under his jurisdiction.

Noor moved hastily to Suresnes, where she had spent her childhood. Her old friends there were more surprised than overjoyed at seeing her after she explained her reason for returning to France. She had her orders from London to "lie low!" And she did.

In mid-September, Noor moved back into the city, leasing a flat on the Rue de la Faisanderie. It was close by 84 Avenue Foch, Gestapo headquarters. Whether this proximity was courted intentionally by Noor—to be better able to watch the enemy—she did not indicate to co-workers.

Reestablishing radio communications with faraway Baker Street, Noor endeavored to list those agents who had not been caught during the course of a disastrous summer. In these bleak days when the secret police, if not necessarily the Wehrmacht, seemed to be operating without challenge, none could have foreseen that captive Paris would be free just one year later.

The last week of September, Noor was advised that a Lysander was arriving to return her to London. She said she preferred to remain at the Rue de la Faisanderie until she was certain of a relief wireless operator. By the time this was arranged, the moon had waned—no more night landings.

In mid-October, Noor was arrested in her flat. She had, it was believed, been betrayed by the sister of a couple working for the Maquis, who lived in her apartment building.

"Madeleine" was no easy prisoner. She bit one of her captors, who was a collaborator, so hard that he screamed and
blood flowed. It pleased the Gestapo men, who held scant
affection for French traitors.

They weren't so amused when Noor fled through a fifth-
floor bathroom window at 84 Avenue Foch. She raced like a
specter across rooftops, past successive sooty chimney pots
of Paris before she was recaptured.

Stürmbahnführer Kieffer himself was to attest that Noor
"behaved most bravely . . . and we got absolutely no new
information out of her at all."

Her wardens reasoned, incorrectly enough, that the lovely
Indian-English-American girl would not try again. They had
lost sight of the fact that among other prisoners brought
subsequently into Avenue Foch was a suave master British
agent and artist by profession, Captain John Starr. "Bob," as
the "org" knew him, could have substituted at any time for
David Niven or James Mason and their gentlemanly international spy roles.

The Nazis themselves were so impressed with Starr's
varied skills that they set him to work repairing vacuum
cleaners and other mechanical equipment at Gestapo headquarters—and trusted him with a set of tools. He, of course,
took a screwdriver or two back to his cell.

Noor, together with a third prisoner, a French Colonel
Lucien Faye, and Starr shared the implements in removing
the skylights over their respective cells. They made ropes
from blankets and sheets.

They fled once more, over the roofs, after Starr had
left a taunting letter to Kieffer, concluding, "wishing you the
best of luck in the chase that will follow, but much better
luck to ourselves. . . . Bob."

The Germans were lucky. A sudden air raid brought extra soldiers and searchlights out into the thundering night. The trio was captured in a nearby house.

That was it. Noor Inayat Khan was hustled onto a train and taken to prison in Pforzheim. There she was chained to a wall—and spent most of her confinement in this cruel position.

The manacling was unnecessary. The stark German camp was virtually escape-proof, especially for women prisoners. For two months, the Indian "princess's" wireless kept transmitting from Paris to London. It had been seized in her apartment, together with codes and copies of messages, both those sent and received.

The Germans tagged this operation "Diana," but although the sender was able to answer a surprising number of identifying questions about Noor and her family, Baker Street never was convinced of "Diana's" authenticity.

Noor might have seen the war through at Pforzheim, in her chains and out of them. However, a woman attendant at nearby Karlsruhe prison pondered why a number of female prisoners—including German criminals and political pariahs—appeared to be permanent boarders both there and at Pforzheim. Either to curry favor or merely as the act of a compulsive busybody, this warden voiced her wonderings to the regional Gestapo chieftain, an otherwise nobody named Joseph Gmeiner.

Gmeiner knew that Kieffer was completing many trips from Paris to Karlsruhe in spite of the obvious difficulties of transportation. Even so, Gmeiner thought not too much of this, since Kieffer's family lived in Karlsruhe. It never occurred to Gmeiner that his fellow SS director was making every effort to keep his prisoners alive—not because he liked them or was bursting with human kindness, but because it suited his counterintelligence needs. He was also sticking to his part of the pact.

(As a matter of fact, Kieffer's solicitude paid off. Convicted by the Court of the Seine, after the war, close to the scenes of his activities, and sentenced to death, he was reprieved. Gmeiner's justice seemed more appropriate. He was hung.)

Gmeiner telephoned Berlin. What to do with these prisoners, especially the English "swine"?

He must wait—say, an hour or two—while "disposition" officers checked with the deceptively mild-appearing Heinrich Himmler. He had mercilessly eliminated all rivals within Nazi hierarchy to assume unchallenged command of the SS, the SA, the dreaded Gestapo, in fact all of the secret police, military and civilian, as well as certain "elite" troops not necessarily charged with intelligence or counterintelligence activities.

The answer from the bespectacled, soft-spoken Himmler was casually familiar, also devoid of any emotion: "Kill them."

Four women were removed from Karlsruhe and shoved onto a train bound westward for Natzweiler, in Alsace. Natzweiler was designated, in the Nazi sense of methodical organization, among whatever other its purposes, as an extermination camp.

The group selected included "Denise," the charming French nurse who had been arrested shortly after Noor had joined the "Prosper" team; Diana Rowden ("Paulette"),* the twenty-nine-year-old yachting enthusiast who had accompanied Noor to France; vivacious Vera Leigh, forty-one

---

* "Alice," Cecily Lefort, who had landed with her, was executed at Ravensbruck.

("Simone"), dress designer as well as bon vivant in London and Continental society; and plump, appealing Sonia Olchanesky, twenty-one, a French-Polish dancer.

They had been told variously that they were to work in an agricultural camp or in the kitchens of Natzweiler, an all-male prison camp. They arrived in the late afternoon, were given a supper of coffee and bread, and were taken to a small examination room in the camp crematorium building. There, the camp's SS doctor, Werner Rohde, himself newly arrived, prepared to inoculate the women, one by one, with deadly phenol.

When one of the condemned asked "Pour quoi?" Rohde was heard to reply, "Pour typhus." The four were cremated shortly after their executions. (Two years later, a British war crimes court found Rohde guilty of "violation of the laws and usages of war." He was hung.)

Noor Inayat Khan and three companions were treated to a rail journey, in a comfortable, overstuffed, second-class coach compartment, past a picturesque section of countryside, southeast through Bavaria. The Swabian Mountains were colorful with early autumn foliage.

The forest cover was bright, an alternating display of white and lavender flowers which thrive at altitude. The scene was part of the fairyland inspiration of four-color posters displayed in the world's travel bureaus almost up to the moment of invasion in September, 1939—and invariably inviting to those voluble tourists who repeated, "Well, at least he [Hitler] doesn't have any unemployment, and he [Mussolini] is making the trains run on time!"

Noor was en route, not to Natzweiler, but to another camp of much the same reputation—Dachau, near Munich—Munich, the birthplace of the Brown Shirts and the National

Socialist terror, Munich the fabled spa of Gemütlichkeit and post-Renaissance churches which now had become identified with a twentieth-century Dark Ages.

This bright, beautiful September 11, the four made small talk in English (their guards would recall) just like any visitors from across the Channel in happier days. The macabre aspect of the journey, in the waning months of a brutal, devastating war, would have staggered the imagination of a Dante, a Poe, or conceivably a Wagner. How could the grotesque overtones be adequately captured, in faithfully stark dimension?

The women chatted, pointed, and even laughed as the minutes sped away, like brittle leaves falling in autumn which can never possibly return. It was as though none knew her true destination or what awaited her there.

With Noor ("Madeleine") were "Martine," "Yvonne," and "Gaby."

"Martine," Madeleine Damerment, a twenty-seven-year-old soft-spoken Lille native, had been betrayed and arrested on her landing near Chartres in February, one of eighteen thus surprised before they had an opportunity for even a minute's work (although some shot, knifed, or slugged their way to safety). Her father, Charles, had died in a concentration camp, although her mother miraculously had survived similar confinement.

In Cell 17, Karlsruhe, a German woman inmate would never forget the half-fictitious tales Madeleine wove of her family and personal biography, also how she used to burst into sobs in the night when her companion thought she had been fast asleep.

". . . Madeleine, lieber Gott, she wanted so much to live!"

"Gaby," in Cell 16, Eliane Plewman, was the "conspicuously attractive" offspring of a British father and Spanish mother. The same age as Madeleine Damerment, Mrs. Plewman, a young woman with dark, brooding eyes, had been a daring courier in the Marseilles area. She had assisted in blocking the main line to Toulon by derailing a train inside a tunnel; also helped knock out at least thirty locomotives.

Bursting boilers in the roundhouses of southern France became a reverberating rumble that was dulcet harmony to the ears of the resistance.

"Yvonne," thirty-three-year-old Swiss-born Yolande Beekman, had made life hell for the Germans along a 115-mile stretch of rail between Paris, St. Quentin, and Lille for nearly a year. "Yvonne" was surely Louise de Bettignies reincarnate.

A wireless operator, Yolande projected herself into side duties of train derailments. She earned the praise of a superior: "Of the finest stuff imaginable!"

All of these ladies were of the same "finest stuff." But that still was not enough when balanced on the German's own overweighted scales, by which they measured life or death.

The four, according to one witness, were permitted to tarry but one night in their Dachau cells. The next morning they were awakened early, offered lukewarm weak tea, ersatz breakfast rolls, and led out, in pairs, across the prison courtyard, toward a wall.

On the well-worn cobblestones before the wall were old, dried bloodstains, already dark brown from sun and weather. The only consideration—each two women were allowed to hold hands as an SS man, with unflinching *sang-froid*, shot them in the back of the neck. The whole bizarre

episode was as casual and impersonal as though the execu-
tioner was firing at clay pigeons.

And so the four died, accorded not even legal formality,
the time to write letters, spiritual comfort, or the dignity,
gruesome enough, of a firing squad as others before them
had been granted. Coming to mind, for example, were Edith
Cavell and Mata Hari.

"Norah," wrote Maurice Buckmaster, SOE section chief in
London and former British automobile executive in Paris,
who called Noor by that name, "behaved throughout with
the greatest bravery and went to her death with that serene
defiance which typified the gallant women of SOE, women
who like Violette Szabo dared everything in the defense of a
cause in which they believed."

Noor's passing also wrote *finis* to the "Prosper" team.
Francis Suttill and Gilbert Norman, who had been tortured,
and interrogated almost without surcease, now lay cold and
broken in their graves. Or their ashes had been swept out
into the chill winds of Bavaria.

None could really say or, within the fraternity of the Gestapo, care.

Just why were Madeleine, Louise, Denise, Simone, Paulette, Jacqueline, Ambroise, Nadine, Alice, Gaby, Yvonne,
Martine, and many others not officially in the "org," bearing
forgotten names and certainly forgotten faces, singled out
for the conqueror's most earnest venom?

None was a "master spy" in the fictional cloak-and-dagger
tradition who purloined the enemy's highest war secrets.
Was it but the contemptuous and consistently unrelenting
defiance of these women which so angered their captors that
they had unavoidably signed their own death warrants?

If but one woman of SOE had been slain, it would have

been shame enough. Actually, some three times the number executed survived, although surely this was not because of any change of heart, sudden compassion, or unfamiliar softness of the Nazis.

Several, such as Yvonne Rudellat, died in concentration camp or after their liberation, including, as well, Muriel Byck ("Violette") and Madeleine Lavigne ("Isabelle").

Christine Granville, who, as the Countess Krystyn Gizycka Skarbek, had been a Polish beauty queen, was an exceptionally talented and busy spy, working first in Poland, then in France, eastern Europe, and finally North Africa. Arrested twice, she nonetheless managed to be set free each time. She survived the war to be murdered in 1952 in London by a jealous suitor.

French-born Odette Marie Sansom, small, dark-haired, accomplished the unusual by receiving the George Cross herself rather than posthumously. She was thirty when in October, 1942, she was landed in southern France as the agent "Celine," or "Lise."

She linked up at a Salon de Beaute in Cannes with her team commander, "Raoul," who was in fact Captain Peter Morland Churchill, the dashing leader of the southern group of the French resistance, no relation to the Prime Minister.

"Raoul" put "Lise" to work as a courier. Her intelligence and tenacity plus her knowledge of French made her especially useful in arranging aerial pickups of agents and night ammunition drops. When Churchill was called back to Baker Street, she supervised their biggest drop yet: to the Maquis hiding out in the mountains above the Cote d'Azur.

It was her last operation before being captured, in April, 1943, on the very morning Churchill was parachuted back into France. One of Kieffer's assistants, SS Sergeant Hugo

Bleicher, arrested "Lise," next "Raoul," in the same inn at Annecy. They had agreed to maintain they were married, and to this story Odette clung through numerous interrogations. Torture such as that meted Noor Inayat Khan failed to elicit from her the names of their wireless operator and another British officer passionately sought by the Gestapo. Starving produced no more effective results.

When Odette was informed she would be shot, her captors enumerated several charges in the dark milieu of espionage, sabotage, and the unforgivable dual sins of being a Frenchwoman and possibly married to an Englishman.

"You must take your pick of the counts," Odette answered her accusers calmly. "I can die only once."

Removing her from Fresnes outside Paris to solitary confinement in the women's prison of Ravensbruck, the Nazis never could work up their courage to execute her. Their suspicious minds clung to the possibility that she, as well as "Raoul," was related to Winston Churchill.

While being shunted around German prisons, Odette was at one time or another traveling companion to Yolande Beekman or adjoining cellmate of Madeleine Damerment as well as Eliane Plewman. In the quiet hours of the night, when not interrupted by screamings of other prisoners, the women whispered messages back and forth. One of their number—just possibly—might survive to carry these final thoughts and wishes to England, or to a free France.

Odette's luck held. Fritz Sühren, commandant of Ravensbruck, drove her in his black Mercedes to the thundering American lines in May, 1945. The Reich's total surrender was but two weeks distant. He was at once taken prisoner by the liberating armies after Odette had demanded and obtained his revolver—a memento of the darkest months of her life.

If the cocky, blond SS officer had hoped this gallantry, perhaps the sole act of gallantry in his entire life, would win him clemency, he was mistaken. A war crimes court decided it was too late for him to evince humanity. However, to the moment he took his last steps to the gallows he was accorded all the rights, physical and spiritual, of the condemned—human consideration in extremis he had never lavished on his own charges.

The citation accompanying Odette's George Cross read, in part:

". . . she also drew Gestapo attention from her commanding officer onto herself, saying that he had only come to France on her insistence. She took full responsibility and agreed that it should be herself and not her commanding officer who should be shot. By this action she caused the Gestapo to cease paying attention to her commanding officer after only two interrogations.

"In addition, the Gestapo were most determined to discover the whereabouts of a wireless operator and of another British officer whose lives were of the greatest value to the resistance organization. Mrs. Sansom was the only person who knew of their whereabouts. The Gestapo tortured her most brutally to try to make her give away this information. They seared her back with a red-hot iron and, when that failed, they pulled out all her toe-nails. Mrs. Sansom, however, continually refused to speak, and by her bravery and determination she not only saved the lives of the two officers but enabled them to carry on their most valuable work.

"During the period of her two years in which she was in enemy hands, she displayed courage, endurance and self-sacrifice of the highest possible order."

As in the storybooks, Odette married her "pretend husband" of the perilous espionage days: Peter Churchill. However, unlike the same books, they did not exactly live happily ever after. The courageous "Lise" of SOE fame is now Mrs. Geoffrey Hallowes, of London.

A surprisingly large number of women eluded capture completely—a youthful blonde English girl, for example, with the Saturday matinee-sounding name, Pearl Witherington. Her *code nom de plume*, "Marie," carried a banal ring, by comparison.

She was dropped into France in September, 1943.

"I had been sent on a job which I was told would not be easy," Pearl would recall, "because I was not known to the people I was to contact. Neither was there a password. I was told to say I was calling on behalf of 'Robert.'

"When I arrived, my contact was away in another town, so I told his wife I would be back at the same time next day. As soon as I walked into the *estaminet* (small cafe) the second time, I realized I was in for a spot of trouble by the expression on the wife's face.

"She showed me into a large room where I was greeted by an unknown man, who asked me a few questions. I could see he did not trust me.

"He showed me up a tiny corkscrew staircase into a small room and continued his questioning. Every time he asked me if I knew so-and-so I had to answer 'No!' which was the truth. And when I asked him the same question I got the same answer.

"Things were looking rather bad, so I decided to throw my last card. 'Do you know Octave?' I asked.

" 'No . . .'

" 'Well,' I said. 'His real name is C——. He was caught and imprisoned a short while after I was dropped on his landing ground.'

"To my utter relief, Robert, for that was my questioner's name, said he knew him!

"There was a stir in the room next to the one we were in and from there emerged four strong young men, armed.

"Apparently what happened was a mix up with the name of Robert, for there was another Robert in the town.

"The crux was that my questioner was positive that I was a spy and the five of them had planned to kill me."

Once her initial problem was resolved, Pearl went to work as the top member of a hard-hitting resistance team commanded by Squadron Leader Maurice Southgate. Southgate, a rather improbable Frank Merriwell-Wyatt Earp combination, could not, nonetheless, continue his fabulous game of cowboys and Indians indefinitely.

He was captured (although his luck held through captivity in the notorious Colditz), and Pearl continued his work, with curtain-calling success. She increased the number of "reception committees" for drops of armaments, and also improved upon the quality of their membership.

She organized still more sabotage teams for tying rail traffic into vexing snarls—like the Place de la Concorde or Times Square at rush hour—and taught fighters how to bomb, tear up, and otherwise clutter highways until they resembled obstacle courses on athletic fields. "Marie" was credited with several hundred derailments or severed rights-of-way.

Five days after D-Day, Pearl and 150 French resistance fighters were attacked by more than 2,000 Germans. The battle lasted for fourteen hours. When the Englishwoman's ammunition was spent, she hid in a cornfield, under the parching sun, while machine-gun bullets sliced through the stalks.

"I had to be very careful how I moved," she recalled. "I

watched the heads of the corn above me and when they stirred by the breeze I moved a little closer to the edge of the field. I had to wait until the wind moved the corn, otherwise the Boche would have noticed it moving and fired directly at that spot."

"But they finally gave up and I managed to get away."

Pearl's greatest challenge came in the days after that pitched battle, as citizens of all ages, men and women, volunteered to aid in the fast-developing liberation. She personally organized 1,500 Frenchmen into active, trained, and equipped fighting groups.

All in all, it was not surprising that Pearl fell in love with one of her "pupils," Henri Cornioley, and married him. Mme. and M. Cornioley now live in France.

Yvonne Baseden, shortly after joining the WAAF, in 1940, at the age of eighteen, became the youngest officer in SOE's wireless corps. By the time she was parachuted into France in the spring of 1944, Yvonne (code "Odette," but no relation to Odette Sansom) was experienced in commando tactics and all the advanced niceties of resistance survival that could be taught by her knowledgeable seniors in England.

As "Mlle. Marie Bernier," a secretary, she was an effective radio spy, as she was supposed to be. In addition, she aided materially in delivering resistance material obtained from night drops.

Caught when the Gestapo surrounded a farmhouse GHQ of the Maquis, Yvonne hid under a pile of fuel logs in the kitchen. She believed she had been undetected until, after more than an hour, she was yanked out literally by the hair and taken, manacled to Ravensbruck.

Upwards of 100,000 women had now perished in this

charnel house of prisoners of all nationalities, including German. The latter's crimes were more often than not merely disaffection for the Nazi cause.

Yvonne Baseden was treated badly, even by the low standards of this place of abysmal inconsideration. She was starved, abandoned in a cramped, dark cell for days, and once taken before an execution wall and fired at by a squad whose orders were to miss. Still, the young Yvonne had nothing to tell her captors and torturers. They stamped on her toes with their heavy army boots and again threatened to kill her. They put her in a hut with eight hundred sick women, including those who were pregnant and yet others accompanied by their emaciated babies. Her rations, as those for the others, were a bowl or so of carrot or marigold soup a day and ersatz bread, the ingredients of which were largely sawdust.

At about the same time of April, 1945, as Violette Szabo, Denise Bloch, and Lillian Rolfe were shot, Yvonne Baseden was released—at the importunings of the Swedish Red Cross.

The ability to melt anonymously into even a medium-sized crowd was thirty-two year-old Lise de Baissac's greatest life insurance.

When first parachuted into France late in 1942, with Andrée Borrel, she was masquerading as a poor, black-clad widow, "Mme. Irene Brisse." She borrowed a bicycle from a priest in Poitiers, on the road from Bordeaux to Paris, in order to hunt rock specimens and bird eggs. Or so her story went.

The Germans ignored this plain, unfortunate-looking creature. For eleven months she was busy collecting, not eggs or rocks, but tons of guns and ammunition fluttering out of the night skies, consigned to the Maquis. Her ears were ever open for careless pieces of conversation from German soldiers on strength and probable positioning of their forces.

In August, 1943, Lise returned by plane to England. On board was another homebound agent, and one she knew very well: her brother.

She broke her leg in parachute practice, which delayed her second visit to occupied France. Just before D-Day, Lise arrived in Normandy, as "Mme Janet Banville." The "elderly widow," a role in which she had become adept, now taught subjects hardly expected of the character she portrayed. She trained recruits to the resistance in the use of a Sten gun, the niceties of self-defense including tripping so as to fracture a shinbone, choking or even garroting an enemy sentry.

Once a German patrolman grabbed at her bicycle with the guttural command, "Give that to me!"

She pulled away from him and slapped him in the face, resisting the impulse to seriously injure or perhaps even kill him with a bruising blow to the throat.

"How dare you!" she cried.

In her abrupt move, parts of her wireless transmitter, tied to her legs, clattered onto the ground and shattered. The German had been so taken by surprise that he strode off without even noticing the incriminating evidence.

When eight members of the Wehrmacht were billeted in her house, Lise was certain that she would be found out, later confessing, "I was scared." Fortunately, June 6 had come and gone. The Nazis were in retreat.

Her fellow boarders left one morning even more quickly

than they had checked in. And the same afternoon, Lise unpacked her Women's Transport Service uniform, which had been carefully hidden under the rafters.

When the first GI's trudged by her yard, Lise, proud and resplendent in her uniform, saluted her Allied liberators—Lise de Baissac who looked so commonplace that no one really could believe anything clandestine or especially exciting about her.

Then, there was Nancy Wake, an Australian girl who helped one thousand Allied soldiers and young Frenchmen on their way to England. Nancy survived to wave the Union Jack at the liberating armies marching into Paris, although her French husband was slain.

And Peggy Smith, train wrecker extraordinary. Also Kitty Bonnefois, who hid more than 135 men in her Paris flat at various times before being herself arrested.

The Boston-born Countess Roberta de Mauduit made available to the resistance her centuries-old castle in the Cotes-du-Nord, near the Channel, after her husband had set sail in a fishing smack for De Gaulle's forces in England. When finally "Betty," as her friends knew her, was seized by the Gestapo, five American airmen were still hiding under a double floor in the attic.

The pretty Countess was taken to prison, where she remained for two years, until the end of the war. Her five "guests" had long since made good their escape.

Among Betty de Mauduit's many decorations were the George Cross and the American Medal of Honor.

The list of women who worked and not only fought side-by-side with the men but often led the way for them could go on. They were an indispensable part, first, of the defensive, then, as they grew bolder and stronger, the offensive.*

General Eisenhower joined Churchill and other leaders in attributing significant credit for the Allied victory to the men and women who not only tied down whole Nazi (and sometimes Fascist) divisions but made it increasingly difficult for their front-line forces to get there.

Peter Churchill, "Raoul," in his memoirs, *Duel of Wits,* alluded to the seemingly disproportionate cost of supreme patriotism as expressed by civilian warfare: "Resistance movements took a larger share . . . than is generally realized, the French losing in the region of 200,000 people in the concentration camps and the heroic Poles topping the tragic list with a death toll twice as great as the total losses incurred by the combined Armed Forces of the United States for the whole war (slightly more than 291,000)."

The task of singling out anyone for his or her acts of bravery is overwhelming, if not wholly impossible. Nor is it any easier to focus on the sacrifice of one individual British woman. Plaques in memory of some of these heroes, such as that at Knightsbridge, London, only hint at the story.

The years have fled. Tears are dry. But so long at least as memory exists, there will live, too, Britain's *heroine* of World War II.

Time, the leveler, the equalizer, the master artist of perspective, has created from many a single, immortal image.

---

* See the next chapter for the tarnished side of valor, the story of Britain's "nonheroines."

7

⁝

TRAITORS AND CRACKPOTS

➻ *Britain's Nonheroines of World War II*

Among the "nonheroines" of Britain in World War II—the traitors, the enemy agents, and the crackpots—was a forty-two-year-old boardinghouse keeper on the Isle of Wight. Plump and nondescript, Mrs. Dorothy Pamela O'Grady had long lived in untrammeled anonymity in Sandown, on the eastern, Channel-side coast.

Home guardsmen first noticed Pamela wandering around prohibited beach areas at night. She flashed her electric torch and acted in other ways to draw attention upon herself. What was this otherwise very "average" boardinghouse ma'am up to?

Scotland Yard was summoned to the small island hitherto associated only with yachting. Agents placed her under close surveillance. Finally she was arrested while attempting to cut telephone wires leading westward to Cowes, then to the mainland of England across the Solent.

At this time, after the fall of France, the British Isles were threatened momentarily with invasion. Was Mrs. O'Grady working with the enemy? Or was she merely an odd one? The detectives, certain that this strange woman in her early middle years was but one of some kind of sabotage group, brought her before the local magistrate. He was not convinced that she meant anything dire. A bomb or two had fallen on the island. Its citizens were under tension. After all, the Nazi hordes could be expected to storm ashore first at this handy beachhead.

"Have a good rest," he admonished Mrs. O'Grady, imposing a small fine of a few pounds.

Pamela O'Grady now moved across the island, to Yarmouth on the west coast. Scotland Yard, persisting in the official belief that there was something very sinsister about the boardinghouse keeper, posted a twenty-four-hour watch over her comings and goings.

She did not flash lights any more or try to sever telephone lines. But her actions remained out of the "norm." She formed a habit, for example, of making trips up the Solent on the ferry to Southampton, where she met with successive individuals, who might well have been strangers to her.

In a few weeks, she was rearrested. This time, documents "of military importance" were found on her. After a secret trial, the judge decided the papers were of sufficient "importance" (although their nature was not publicly revealed) for a very severe penalty indeed—to be "hung by the neck until dead." It was, in marked contrast to the cattlelike slaughter of women in Germany, the only death sentence imposed in England during the war.

But Mrs. O'Grady was not hung. Her sentence, on appeal, was commuted to fourteen years penal servitude. Finally released in 1950, Mrs. O'Grady talked volubly. The whole affair was a big joke, she insisted. Her husband, a fireman, had gone off to war; she was left by herself, save for her dog, a black retriever, Rob, whom she took for nightly swims.

Mrs. O'Grady was lonely. She wished to attract attention to herself: "I longed to be arrested." Once she realized her wish: "I looked forward to the trial as a huge thrill".

She had read too much spy fiction, mingled with some fact. She envisioned herself awakened at dawn—a British Mata Hari, though no dancer—to face a firing squad. Mrs. O'Grady admitted her first "disappointment" was the judge's pronouncement of hanging, for "what's the good of being hanged if I can't see what's happening?"

Mrs. O'Grady survived her self-styled "joke" to confess her exhibitionist impulses. But when she reentered the world of free people, her "joke" backfired several times. Nobody really believed her story. To her surprise, her old friends ostracized her. They turned on their heels when she sought to greet them. Once again, Dorothy Pamela O'Grady found herself adrift in a lonely world, pondering what she would do *this* time to attract attention.

While Mrs. O'Grady was flashing lights seaward and throwing sticks into the Channel waters for Rob to fetch, another Briton, a hairdresser of Dundee in her mid-fifties, was already serving a four-year prison sentence. Mrs. Jesse Jordan had an early start in the business of espionage.

Her undoing was the volume of international mail building up in 1938 to and from her shabby little beauty parlor at 1 Kinloch Street. The local postman, try as he might over his evening 'alf-and 'alf, just could not understand why Mrs. Jordan would have so many friends in the United States, South America, Mexico, Germany, Italy, Spain, and even Japan.

British military intelligence, MI-5, obligingly cut in the

FBI on the mystery. After a few weeks of steaming and copying her mail, not much mystery remained.

A German spy ring, headquartered in New York, was found to be using Mrs. Jordan simply as a central address. The setup was quite agreeable to the hairdresser; her husband was a German who had been killed in 1918. Although English-born, she had lived or traveled in Germany so much that her accent persisted as markedly "foreign." Jesse's community, except on a coldly professional plane, never really accepted her.

She was found guilty in that "at a place in Fife being a prohibited place she did make a sketch or plan thereof—calculated to be directly or indirectly useful to an enemy." It was further charged that she plotted the locations of Scottish Coast Guard stations and other mappings calculated to be "useful to an enemy bomber."

Eighteen of her correspondents, some in absentia, were indicted in New York, including two attractive German women, Katie Moog and Johanna Hofmann. They were charged with a remarkable list of accomplishments, including the obtaining of blueprints for devices in aircraft carriers, new depth bombs, fighter plane designs, United States military and diplomatic code books, maps, and other supposedly secret matter.

Still, this was not wartime in America, nor yet across the Atlantic, even though German troops were rolling into Austria the very March afternoon of Mrs. Jordan's arrest. The defendants were given either relatively mild prison sentences or deported. They were far luckier than their countrymen who, a few years later, would find the electric chair ready when they landed as saboteurs from German U-boats.

Fortunate, too, was the thirty-eight-year-old White Russian "Baroness" Anna Wolkoff, who seduced a very junior clerk in the American embassy in London. Tyler Gatewood Kent, rather handsome in a frozen sculptured sort of way, at least ten years Anna's junior, went along with her request for certain diplomatic papers largely because of the pair's mutual dislike of Jews, or those they merely believed to be Jewish.

The whole case was so tritely improbable, so seemingly contrived, that only the tawdriest of pulp magazines would have considered it even as a piece of detective fiction. Tall, curly-haired Tyler Kent was the scion of an old, respected family and offspring of a onetime ambassador to the imperial Czarist court. As a lad he ran like a muscled deer on the athletic field and mastered so many subjects in his fashionable Washington preparatory school, including Latin, that even the erudite headmaster, Dr. William Church, was scarcely qualified to grade him.

He went on to Princeton, then the Sorbonne, and emerged speaking fluently at least four languages, to enter the foreign service. Seemingly in his parent's footsteps, he was even sent to Moscow, although no longer was Russia imperial, by the wildest of imaginations. Tyler did not find the Bolsheviks sympathetic.

He especially detested Jews. Since he made no secret of it, one might wonder how he had been accepted in the first place as a Department of State employee. He sought out and was welcomed by the extreme right-wing set, extending even into Parliament. Here, apparently, was a friend of Hitler's in the Court of St. James.

Anna Wolkoff was a daughter of an admiral in the Czarist navy, and even if her claim to "Baroness" might have been negotiable, she could not have found a better dupe or straight man by advertising. Tyler Gatewood, as most of his undergraduate contemporaries knew him, was the answer to the prayers of a secret agent.

Like so many exiled White Russians, the "Baroness" held no especial emotion for the Fuehrer or the Nazis. Her anti-Semitic feelings were her own. Anna rationalized in a cold and twisted fashion that she could use the Third Reich as a tool for revenge, even though she was a naturalized British subject.

She had arranged with Berlin at the outbreak of war to convey any information which might come to her attention pertaining to America's intentions of becoming a belligerent. It was a ripe field for speculation.

Somewhat like Velvaleee Dickinson, Anna Wolkoff used an obscure store as a front—in this case a London dress shop. Talented, she also painted beautiful water colors, some of which she sold at a good price, but most she gave to her friends.

It was inevitable that Anna and Tyler Gatewood should meet, as they did, at one of the many ultraconservative soirées of their fascist or neofascist set.

The war was a "Jewish conspiracy," she said, was it not? Anna's words were like a love elixir to the young American. "Of course" it was. He could have told her as much long ago.

When she cooed that she could show him how they both, working together, could shorten the war and, some way or other, deprive the "profiteers" of further aggrandizement, Tyler Gatewood was a bumbling, altogether malleable Antony in her hands.

All he had to do was to copy down as much of the State Department–American embassy correspondence as he could and deliver it to her. In fact, he need not tire himself by taking this and that tram route to her flat. She would gladly go to his. As a reward, she would leave him freshly brushed water colors, and conceivably other favors, depending on both mood and, of course, cooperation.

Tyler Gatewood, wittingly enough, translated and had microfilmed 1,500 confidential, secret, and restricted cables and letters from Washington. Many were of the Roosevelt-Churchill exchange, potentially of a very compromising nature. In so doing, though he likely had no such intent, Kent also betrayed the currently in force U.S. diplomatic code to an ever more probable enemy: Germany.

Apparently Kent never considered that Scotland Yard could scarcely fail to keep tabs on a known White Russian who, since the early months of the war and in increased tempo during the Battle of Britain, was keeping company, in ultraconservative circles, with a member of the foreign diplomatic corps.

The well-matched pair of bigots were arrested in 1940 in Kent's flat after they were traced through the photographer who did the microfilming. Ambassador Joseph P. Kennedy, both embarrassed and infuriated, told reporters: "If America had been at war, I would have recommended that Kent be sent back to America and shot as a traitor." State Department encoders, now working overtime to change their books, agreed only in part. They thought he should be shot anyhow.

His Majesty's courts, deciding that nothing really "vital" had been transmitted to Berlin—fortunately—sentenced Anna to ten years imprisonment, Tyler Kent to seven. He was paroled in December, 1945, returning to the United States to continue preaching his philosophies, or rather, antiphilosophies. Anna, released the following year, found herself in a curious, wholly unenviable position. Stripped of her British citizenship and necessarily undesirable to Soviet Russia, Miss Wolkoff became a woman without a country— even without a lover in the American embassy.

There were smaller fish, women such as Norah Lavinia Briscoe, forty, or Gertrude Blount Kiscox, thirty, who pleaded guilty in British Criminal Court to "doing an act likely to assist the enemy in communicating unauthorized information." The rather involved charges arose from pure ignorance of mail censorship laws and garrulous musings on paper to friends overseas.

British women throughout the war served time for just such improprieties, and afterward none could say positively if they were wilful or careless.

Whatever the genesis of their misdemeanors, these females surely had become their country's nonheroines of World War II—even as the United States had its own quota, both during and after the war.

But that's another story, and another book.

8

⁝

SPY FROM ON HIGH
·•▸ *Barbara Slade, 1943*

The little things continued their disproportionate influence on the outcome of battle and, sometimes, the course of war: an inconspicuous Quaker Lady whom none associated with espionage, a widow who vowed revenge upon one of the South's great cavalry leaders, a young woman of Lille who tied down platoons of the Kaiser's troops and counterintelligence agents.

In 1943, a WAAF's previous boredom with KP duty combined with unusually sharp eyesight to help her remove much of the sting from one of the war's deadliest weapons.

Barbara Slade fought not with Sten guns and grenades but with high-powered magnifiers, protractors, stereoscopes, and complicated tables for relating distance and size throughout all dimensions. When war came, Barbara was living near Maidenhead about thirty-five miles west of London, on the banks of the Loddon, a private and quiet river which is a tributary of the Thames. As most young women, she wanted to do her part. But what might that be?

She had studied shorthand and typing in business school, before that fine art and also commercial art. Barbara was an accomplished equestrienne and could fish with the best Izaak Waltons.

But she was a pessimist. She did not consider that any of these skills or hobbies qualified her as "of much use" to the forces. She signed up for the WAAF, resigned to accepting any duty that came along. It seemed that the WAAF could have put this charming, talented young brunette to more appropriate service, but she was assigned as mess attendant at the Harwell airfield, on the lonely, windswept Berkshire downs.

"It was the hardest, coldest winter I had ever experienced," she recalled. "We lived four in a room in a new airmen's married quarters but they were very damp, having not dried out properly. We slept on three planks on trestles with straw palliasses [mattresses].

"When the weather turned exceptionally cold after Christmas, we suffered an enforced six weeks confined to camp. We were snowed in and frozen up. Nothing worked in our quarters and we were extremely uncomfortable. Still, we had to report at 6 A.M. for mess duty and with only a short afternoon break we often went through till 10 P.M. on duty.

"It was a new life but one learnt a lot especially from the old mess retainers who were prepared to show us the best way of doing a job in prewar days: shoe cleaning, glass care, silver polishing, etc.

"All food was handed round to the officers in separate dishes and there were at least five courses though fortunately coffee was served in the anteroom."

Spilling soup down the neck of a future air marshal and

taking a tub bath in the village pub (the only hot water offered publicly in Harwell) stood out as sharply etched moments in Barbara's war with the Third Reich that bleak winter.

Partly because of her disenchantment with kitchen and related chores, partly because her talents ultimately *had* to be discovered—even by the military—she was transferred to navigational duties in 1940. The plotting board and its instruments bore recognizable relationship to her art easel.

A year in this improved duty, "more or less comfortable apart from a few stray bombs around the aerodrome," led to a course in a subject still more provocative. A select class of thirty students, men and women of all ages and representing many skills, professions, and avocations, were given a crash course in the increasingly vital science of photo interpretation.

"The unit," as she has recalled (to me) "in fact was an astonishing crowd containing a high proportion of university lecturers, schoolmasters, geologists, and almost all the younger eminent archaeologists."

Graduates were armed with "a large wooden case which contained all the equipment necessary for an interpreter, with a warning not to lose any of it since we should have to refund it from our pay." That was the equivalent of ten dollars a week.

In September 1941 Barbara reported for duty at RAF Medmenham. She was, therefore, still in the Thames Valley and living much the same distance from London.

Hints of a terrible new Nazi weapon soon became insistent. The reports centered on an experimental station at Peenemunde on the Baltic, due south of Sweden. High-altitude and inconclusive photographs revealed earthworks and strange shadows on the barren terrain that whispered "rockets."

It was not then known, but a prototype rocket—the A-4—had soared to a height of fifty miles from Peenemunde in October, 1942. A few weeks later, the fruits of further aerial reconnaissance arrived at Medmenham.

"The first I heard of Peenemunde," said Barbara, "was one morning while hitch-hiking down to Gloucester on a forty-eight-hour leave. I was going to the home of Madeleine Thwaites, a section officer. She had promised me a view of some badgers if I was prepared to go at dusk and sit opposite a hide and wait till they came out on a cold night. There was also a good chance of some horse riding over the beautiful Cotswolds.

"It was then that she told me that in the late hours of a previous night a pile of photographs had been thrown at her just to see if there was anything of interest to report. This was quite normal. The cream so to speak of a sortie was handed out to the superior interpreters. That is to say, the major ports and aerodromes always of vital importance to the Admiralty and RAF came first. The Army interests were more or less left to the Army experts.

"An interpreter always had to be careful of something new especially when it was unknown territory or there was no previous cover (the results of 'covering' aerial reconnaissance). So much of the interpretation relied on previous cover for a guide and comparison.

"On this particular cover Madeleine had seen what appeared to be an extensive smoke screen starting up. She took the photographs to her duty interpretation officer, Claude 'Bill' Wavell, who was in charge (and an expert on detecting enemy radar sites) and told him of her discovery.

"Since the photographs were of not very good quality and

he knew nothing of the 'ground reports' all he could say was that there was a great deal of activity in this area and that there was smoke rising. He did not feel certain that it was a smoke screen (as indeed it was not, but the blast off from a rocket).

"Madeleine was looking at the very important cover which showed considerable new constructions and other activities: it was on this cover that, later on, they found the V-2's and jet marks and other significant objects."

In February, 1943, intelligence within France sent out vague reports of preparations of "some form of long-range projector . . . to bombard England." Accordingly, Barbara and her co-workers at Medmenham were instructed to scrutinize closely every inch of "covered" French ground, especially factory areas, within 130 miles of London.

"Long-range bombardment weapons of a novel type" had indeed left the blueprint stage. Churchill was himself so concerned that he appointed his son-in-law, Duncan Sandys, to head a committee to ascertain what these reports were all about and, if necessary, organize countermeasures.

Sandys visited Medmenham in May, then returned to London convinced of something "sinister" in the making. "Remotely controlled pilotless aircraft?" Possibly. Right now, neither the portrait nor pedigree of the "sinister" shadows could be established. All the interpreters at Medmenham could do was to continue to "look out for anything unusual" in northern France.

Photo interpretation, the Air Ministry, No. 10 Downing Street, almost all concerned with the defense of England and the defeat of Nazi Germany, believed there were such things as pilotless aircraft. However, photography could not prove it.

In the early summer, the rockets commenced to reveal

themselves. Photographs showed them at Peenemunde, lying on trailers and protected by earthworks. Later on, Constance Babbington-Smith, a WAAF officer in charge of Aircraft and Airfields section made out four tailless airplanes in a Peenemunde negative, presumably in flight. There were scorch or jet marks on the earth.

Here finally unmasked was the "secret weapon to be used against London, an air mine with wings, long-distance steering and rocket drive, launched by catapult." It was speedily labeled "Peenemunde 30," with the additional code name, "Diver."

Now Churchill paid a visit to Medmenham, where he amazed the staff by his familiarity with rockets and the concept of flying bombs. Nor did he seem surprised that the Germans might be ready to loose barrages against England.

It was time to do something about it. On the night of August 17, more than six hundred aircraft were sent against Peenemunde. It was a hazardous thousand-mile round trip from the British Isles to the Baltic. Forty planes were lost in the fierce ground fire and fighter plane protection. Enough damage was caused, however, to convince the enemy to transfer most of the station's functions to the improved sanctuaries of Poland and the Harz Mountains in Germany.

Events moved swiftly. A prototype of the V-1 fluttered down like a great clumsy bird on the Danish island of Bornholm. A very brave Dane indeed discovered it half-buried in the sand and made a report via resistance channels to London. In France, a member of the underground, Michel Hollard, disguised himself as a workman and visited construction sites along the Channel coast. There he found blockhouses, railway tracks, or positions for tracks, leading to steep embankments shored with timbers. When, with a pocket compass, he discovered that the apparent catapult positions pointed toward London, he suspected at once "secret weapons." He reported this to his own contact in Lausanne.

That same August "Bodyline" was increased to include all of the armed forces except the Navy. Douglas Kendall, a brilliant RAF wing commander, was put in charge, and shortly the code name was changed to "Crossbow," of historic familiarity and perhaps relevance. Although men accounted for 80 percent of the staff, Barbara was not alone. Other women included Joan Driver, Pauline Grouse, Ann Tapp and an attractive redhead from Denmark, Diana Jonzen.

"I started targetting the sites, which I got to know very well," said Barbara. Indeed, as one of the men in the section, Robert Bulmer, observed, Barbara developed "an uncanny, almost psychic" aptitude.

They popped up in "cover" photos just as the agent Hollard had reported, all the way from Cherbourg to Calais. By late November the fantastic number of sixty-four "ski" sites —the V-1 launching rails—had been detected, all within 150 miles of London or Portsmouth. The most complete was in the Bois Carré, or "square woods," near Yvrench.

"I became so familiar with these activities," Barbara added, "that I could safely say I was able to identify every site we had targetted including the heavy sites (with exceptionally large reinforced structures, designed for multiple firing) and supply sites, and more or less knew the state of completion. The effectiveness of the photographic cover was clearly shown by the German efforts to avoid detection."

Britain had waited long enough, possibly too long. Bombing began on December 5, 1943, and continued until March 1945. Before January 1, 1944, more than three thousand tons of bombs had been dumped on the "ski" sites. Hitler's time-table for hurling these *Vergeltung*, or vengeance weapons, at England had to be revised. The element of surprise had been irrevocably denied the enemy.

"The last Bois Carré, or 'ski' site," Barbara continued, "was discovered on 21 January 1944 though the search for these and supply sites went on for two months. I was taken on to do interpretation which of course included bomb damage assessment. One of the surprises was that, although the firing sites appeared to be complete, the Germans never put up the rails, but one could see the position they would take on the ground."

Throughout the late winter and spring of 1944, the game of cat and mouse continued. The mouse, furtively it hoped, came from undercover long enough to resume its activity, then the cat pounced. More than twenty thousand tons of bombs were dropped on the "mouse" lairs in this period, at least half again the weight hurled at London during the fall, 1940, to spring, 1941, Blitz.

These were extremely persistent "mice," however, apparently with nine or more lives of their own.

"There was a short lull," said Barbara, "with the successful bombing and then suddenly the modified sites appeared, on 23 April—one of the first clear pictures of this type was at a place called Belhamelin, on the Cherbourg Peninsula. This started the biggest efforts in Crossbow."

The photo laboratory sleuths in Medmenham also discovered that the flying bombs must have a recoverable undercarriage. The reason for this deduction was the presence of trolley marks in front of the ramp or ramp position.

Barbara's section was augmented by fifteen additional interpreters, whose assignment it was to become as familiar

with all of the square acreage in northern France within
150 miles of London, Plymouth, or Southampton as with
their own back yards. Soon 300 sites were under surveillance, even with the certainty that numbers of them were
"hottots," or dummies. By now it was ascertained that it
required exactly 120 days to construct a "ski" site.

The task at Medmenham was killing, certainly a blinding
one. Barbara was measuring her night's work in the thousands of prints. Ann Tapp, between darkness and dawn one
incredible night, actually riffled through and looked at
11,000 prints.

The German Flakregiments, so called, were very busy
indeed.

"With the arrival of D-Day," Barbara continued, "we
didn't lessen our efforts. We still couldn't find a completed
site. The Germans were holding back on the ramp. Perhaps
this was why so many people believed it to be a hoax and
that we should never see a projectile fired.

"I was on duty the night of the eleventh or twelfth of June
(almost a week after the invasion) and it was around 3 A.M.
that I saw it. There was no doubt at all. It wasn't a gantry
used for construction, it wasn't camouflage. It wasn't earth
mounds.

"There had been a lot of false alarms on suspected ramps.
I think I shouted, 'Diver!' (a pre-arranged signal to an-
nounce a V-1 site was ready for firing); anyhow everybody
rushed over and peered through the stereoscope.

"There was great excitement as always happened at
Medmenham when any new discovery was made. This was
more important than most.

"We went back to our photographs and two or three more
were discovered as the most recent cover was searched. Rails

were obviously prefabricated and once the foundation had been made could be put up very fast and it would not be long before the firing started."

A day later, June 13, the first V-1 actually put-putted its way across the Channel and crashed drunkenly in Kent. Another was launched, another . . . finally, the fourth scored. It dived down in Bethnal Green, in the East End of London, demolishing a railroad bridge and killing six people.

Then the barrage was interrupted for two days, inspiring the Crossbow chief to sniff, "It's a damp squib." His tone indicated he thought his whole unit had wasted its time the past months on a weapon which had fizzled.

His feelings were wholly premature. It was a very live, hot "squib," indeed, ready to go off with quite a bang. The bombardment was resumed with a flurry which resulted in 144 of the strange "buzz-bombs" smashing somewhere in the vast London civil defense area. Officials had to admit the new Blitz, even as Berlin crowed:

". . . high-explosive weapons of the highest caliber were thrown in with great success against south and southeastern England and the London area. Damage inflicted was tremendous . . . in this hour every one of you here can be more than thankful that he is here in Berlin instead of in London."

At least, as Barbara noted, the changing launch sites "were easily located by black scorch marks at the end of the firing point. In fact some sites were so concealed that only after firing could they be identified."

About 60 percent of the V-1's launched that June actually hit in the broad London area or the east or Channel coasts. Countermeasures included multiple anti-aircraft batteries, especially behind Dover (bristling finally with nearly eight hundred guns) where many of the buzz-bombs crossed, fighter plane attacks, and balloon barrages as snares.

Supreme Allied Commander Eisenhower ruled that bombing the V-1 sites would take priority over all other targets until they were destroyed.

That historic June a V-2 rocket, fired from the presumed ruins of Peenemunde, went wild and crashed in Sweden. This neutral country, now that it was obvious who was going to win the war, was less neutral. It allowed British intelligence to send the fragments of the rocket back to England for study.

In July, upward of 100 V-1's were hurtling down daily upon the United Kingdom. Citizens watched helplessly as the murderous robots swept overhead, praying that the caprice of the pulse-jet motor would fly it just a tiny bit farther before it cut. When the power did switch off, through exhaustion of its fuel supply, the V-1 plummeted earthward like the flying bomb it was. The concussion was as shattering as it was deafening. The blast effect, laterally, was devastating, as thousands of windows were fragmented far from the impact point.

By late August, launching sites were hurriedly moved to Antwerp and environs. The Allied armies were smashing eastward along the Channel coast with ever increasing acceleration. With the fall of Paris, Barbara was transferred to Versailles to continue her interpretation—now of V-2 launching sites as well. The fearsome rockets were beginning to fall on London with a doomsday crash and rolling thunder.

Early the next spring, prior to the Reich's collapse, there were no longer any sanctuaries for loosing the "vengeance" weapons. The citizens of London need fear no more sudden death from the skies. Old people, whose capacity for endurance had long since been exhausted, rolled up their bedding and packed their teapots to emerge from the shelters where they had spent clammy, molelike existences.

"The bombings were a bit different, don't you know," they would explain. Then, they went below only when the sirens warbled of approaching raids.

While the V-2 held awesome potential for the future, the launchings had started too late. The V-1's had been very effective, in spite of countermeasures. Of the 8,000 launched, 2,300 put-putted through to the target area, killing 5,479 persons and injuring an additional 16,000. More than 23,000 homes had been destroyed and possibly as many as one million more damaged.

As their part in keeping these figures to such proportions, shocking enough, Barbara and her fellow interpreters at Medmenham worked nearly 240,000 man-hours and studied 1,600,000 prints. A total of 363 sites were targetted and 4,000 sorties, primarily photographic, flown.

"Had the attack started early in the year," Duncan Sandys stated in recapitulation, "winter conditions would seriously have reduced the efficiency of our countermeasures. Most serious of all, the bombardment would have lasted much longer and our defenses during the first part of the period would have been far less effective."

"Our intelligence," postscripted Winston Churchill, "had played a vital part. The size and performance of the weapon, the intended scale of attack were known to us in excellent time . . . every known means of getting information was employed, and it was pieced together with great skill."

Once again, woman's role was considerable. Trim young ladies such as Barbara Slade bet their keenness of perception and deduction against the might of the Nazi monster—and won.

Her story, as a matter of fact, had an especially happy

ending. She had not escaped notice in her waitressing days for the RAF. A wing commander, Allen H. Wheeler, did not quickly forget pretty Barbara. They were married after the war, and just to improve their togetherness, he taught her to fly.

Mrs. Wheeler now lives in Berkshire, at the intriguing address, "Whistley Bridge Field, near Twyford"—a silent but implacable enemy of Nazi aggression in World War II.

9

·⫶·

THE WOMAN ON OUR CONSCIENCE
·⟶ *Milada Horakova, 1950*

"We know, feel, and are convinced," declared the gray-haired woman in the prisoner's dock, "that if again we had the opportunity and freedom to act, we would not act otherwise than we have acted throughout our lives, serving these noble ideals of liberty, democracy, social progress, and humanity faithfully, even if this faithfulness is regarded in the new concept as high treason. . . ."

Milada Horakova spoke softly, but with a firm voice as she looked her prosecutor in the eye. The shortish, forty-nine-year-old recent member of Parliament and President of the Council of Czechoslovak Women may have been physically reminiscent of the bespectacled lady across the street, her sister who taught school, or someone encountered along any busy thoroughfare. But the similarity was merely casual.

Dr. Horakova was a most unusual woman. Mother of a sixteen-year-old daughter, she was a social reformer and fighter for democracy almost without peer. Not a "spy" in the sense charged by the Communist court, her work in both the postwar and war years had led her into the dangerous purlieus of intelligence and counterintelligence.

Who was this woman? She was no simple Quaker lady, no naïve product of the Tennessee hills, not quite a Louise de Bettignies, nor indeed a Violette Szabo, a Noor Inayat Khan, nor even an Yvonne Rudellat.

Milada Horakova was different. Her continuing resistance, her intelligence, and counterintelligence activities through two distinct reigns of tyranny placed her efforts on a grand scale. Her goal had never been a single military objective, no matter how strategic at the time, but the salvation of an entire nation.

The sphere which Milada sought to influence was no one embattled area of conflict but an international chunk: the West.

Born in Prague on Christmas day, 1901, Milada was the second child in the family of Cenek Kral, amateur actor and devotee of the theater, singing, and the arts, who endowed his blonde, blue-eyed daughter with a dubious and Quixotic heritage. While he did not literally tilt with windmills, he did operate a small pencil factory in defiant opposition of the Hartmuth pencil gargantua.

Cenek Kral, nonetheless, did so well with his Lilliputian manufacture that he raised not only Milada but her two sisters and brother in relative opulence. They were denied nothing in the early years of the twentieth century.

Milada grew up to be an unusually apt schoolgirl who often surprised her classmates by carrying her pet canary, cage and all, to class with her. Though small, she was strong and solidly built, a reasonably competent athlete in tennis, swimming, or less frequent ski jaunts. She took dancing lessons, played the piano, and sang folk songs in a pleasing tenor. Her friends thought of her as gay and cheerful.

And why shouldn't a young girl in Prague feel happy? It was one of the most beautiful Old World cities, full of parks and gardens, art treasures, and structures, from churches to public buildings, of such varied architecture as to draw tourists from the world over. The Ultava River wound under little stone bridges, picturesquely arched to allow the flow of barge traffic. In winter, the river froze, and the citizenry of all ages could skate over its glimmering surface at a furious pace.

The deep, fluffy snows endowed Prague with an especial fairyland softness and majesty. They whitened the parapets and buttresses of the massive Gothic Cathedral of St. Vitus, which dominated the city, with an aura of venerability wholly in keeping with its centuries. The hourly carillons of the less imposing Church of Our Lady of Loreto rang over the snowy hush of Prague the length and breadth of the vast city.

The first year of the Great War brought tragedy to the Kral family. Milada's baby brother and older sister died late in 1914 during a scarlet fever epidemic ravaging the Balkans. However, before the conflict's end, when Milada was a sophomore at the high school in Sleska ulice, she was pushing an infant sister, Vera, through the rose gardens of Petrin Park or past the shop windows bordering Wenceslaus Square.

Soon, wounded soldiers were limping home. Milada joined the young girls in cheering them and strewing flowers in their path. It was all over out there in the wasteland of slaughter, known and understood only imperfectly as the Western Front. None could say just what it had all been about, or who were truly the victors.

Not long after the Armistice, Milada decided to study

medicine, then just as spontaneously changed her mind in favor of the law. This profession was only somewhat more subscribed to by women than doctoring. Nursing itself was just becoming a serious, trained, or respected calling, only through the gluttonous demands of the war. The martyred Edith Cavell had gone far to haul nursing out of the unscientific, often clumsy ministrations of holy orders. She also popularized it as a career for the daughters of socially prominent families.

Milada enrolled in the old Charles ("Karlova") University in Prague where she grew up intellectually with the fast-maturing republic. In 1923, while still a law student, she met Senator Frantiska Plaminkova, a large, impressive lady who was chairman of the influential Czechoslovak Women's Movement. The acquaintanceship led, four years later when Milada had obtained her law degree, to a job in Prague's Welfare Department.

The same year, 1927, Milada married a young editor at Prague's radio station. Bohuslav Horak was a big man with granite features, as physically imposing in his own masculine fashion as Senator Plaminkova was in hers. In various ways, the phlegmatic Bohuslav complemented the emotional qualities of his wife and was balance for her constant striving and her virtually boundless idealism.

During the early 1930's, Milada's work in social welfare was divided into three distinct areas: the problems of children, including orphans and child labor; women's rights; and the special challenges of unemployment created by these depression years. Her innate compassion and desire to help made her an ideal social worker. However, she was peculiarly fitted, through her legal training and linguistic ability, to move even farther afield. And she did.

Acquaintanceship in her work with such leaders in the social sciences as Dr. Petr Zenkl and Rose Pelantova led ultimately to her meeting Alice Masaryk and then her illustrious father himself, Thomas G. Masaryk, first President of the Republic.

He recognized in Dr. Horakova an excellent emissary for Czechoslovakia. Soon she was representing him at social welfare conferences throughout Europe. Graybeards in international law and politics were particularly impressed with the sharp-eyed little woman from Prague and her "remarkable intelligence in perception and judgment, and great promptness in argumentation."

These were years of undiminished accomplishment for Milada, and success. Her only opposition, from a negative standpoint, arose from the small Communist party, more noisy and bothersome than it was consequential. The whole responsibility for unemployment, as one example, the Communists laid at the government's doorstep. Now, if *they* had been in power . . .

In 1933, Milada had cause for her first real sadness since the war years when she lost her brother and sister. Her mother died of cancer, leaving young Vera in her adult sister's care. The same year, however, Milada herself bore a daughter: Jana.

War clouds, even as in 1912–1913, gathered in the 1930's. Soon they towered and darkened into menacing thunderheads. The western border strip, the Sudetenland, home of mixed nationality, as was most of Czechoslovakia, was surrendered at Munich in September, 1938—primarily by British Prime Minister Neville Chamberlain. They were all Germans in the Sudetenland, screamed Hitler, who demanded "Anschluss" with the Vaterland.

This was but overture to greater tragedy coming.

"In the spring," Milada predicted, "we will have Hitler in our castle. I see already SS units marching through the streets of Prague. There will be war. We have to prepare the evacuation of the women and children."

The familiar faces themselves were changing. Masaryk had died the previous year, 1937. He had been succeeded in 1935 by a little known university professor, Dr. Edouard Benes.

The ink was scarcely dry on the Munich "pact" before Milada and other patriots commenced to organize for the dual purpose of resistance and preserving Czech democracy for the future, should worse come to worst. It seemed as though it would.

The apex of the groups was the so-called Political Center, patterned on the structure of the first republic. Its leader was Dr. Zdanek Peska, a prominent newspaper editor.

Milada herself was active in "Verni Zustaneme" ("We shall Remain Faithful"), or, simply, the "PVVZ." Composed of Social Democrats, variously called trade unionists, this "fraternity" possessed a nucleus of forty-five members who set out to draw up a declaration of independence and bill of rights to be tagged, "For Liberty," and authored principally by Milada.

The document, too, was revealing as to just *why* a lawyer and social worker had veered onto the wholly unfamiliar course of resistance, and inevitably into the complexities of international intelligence and counterintelligence.

Then, early on March 15, 1939, Milada was awakened by the ringing of the telephone in her modernly furnished apartment in the Smichov section, overlooking Prague. Her caller was Rose Pelantova.

"Milada," Rose said, "the German army has crossed the border. It will be in Prague in a few hours!"

Few who knew Milada could have believed she would then burst into tears. This emotional giveaway seemed so out of character with her strength, exemplified by her spectacles, severely combed, short hair, conservative dark blue or dark brown dresses with the merest hint of a white collar.

Hitler's euphemistic agreement with Chamberlain had lasted a whole six months. The Fuehrer coveted not merely the Sudetenland strip but all of Czechoslovakia—and more besides.

President Benes had resigned in abject frustration after Munich to be succeeded by a lawyer and relative nobody, Emil Hacha. The only claim to distinction of this long-time compromiser appeared to rest on his translation, some years past, of the whole of Kipling's jungle stories into Czech. Hitler, however, was not interested in linguistic prowess when he brought the sixty-seven-year-old chief of state to Berlin for a predawn meeting.

The Fuehrer spoke with menace. Czechoslovakia must be absorbed within the Third Reich or it would be "annihilated." There was no other choice, *natürlich.*

Pale and shaken, Hacha conceded that "the fate of the Czech people and country [is] in the hands of the Fuehrer of the German Reich."

The elderly statesman apparently felt such personal confidence at being in the "hands" of Hitler that he thereupon fainted. Some reported he fainted again after being revived, rather unceremoniously by a dash from a seltzer bottle in the face.

The conclave had been held at 4:00 A.M. Two hours later, the Wehrmacht was pounding toward Prague as fast as its gray-green lorries, half-tracks, and tanks could roar. The following day, Bohemia and Moravia were annexed to the Reich. Slovakia was taken under "protection." Its "protector" was Konrad Henlein, leader of the Sudeten Nazi party, but otherwise a nobody who had entered the ranks of rabble-rousing from the obscurity of gymnastic teaching. The fiercely national "model" republic which Masaryk had fathered under the encouragement of President Wilson and others at the Versailles Conference had perished after just twenty years of existence.

These developments, whatever their impact upon others of her countrymen, came as a shattering midnight alarm to Milada. First she must find locations: meeting rooms and hideaways for the resistance members. Private homes, apartments, hotels, offices, even hospitals, and churches (with which Czechoslovakia was liberally supplied) all had their place in the organization. And they must be geographically scattered in order to provide the maximum shelter for those who came under enemy surveillance.

In the early months, a great portion of her work involved the widows and children of Czechs deported by the Germans or already executed—trying to obtain news for them, or merely to better what appeared to be threatened destitution. Inevitably in these inquiries she increased her contacts outside of the country, especially in London, which had become the sole European center of effective anti-Nazi resistance, following the fall of France.

Time was running out, however. The work of Milada, through no fault of her own, was too little and too late. PVVZ, although the largest of the resistance groups, was doomed. Its enemies were not only Hitler's Nazis but the traitors within: the Communists, homegrown Fascists, a viper's nest of informers each with his or her own motives, or merely price for betrayal. Hacha himself remained in office as purely a figurehead President, one of Hitler's lower echelon Balkan "protectors."

Cell by cell, member by member, PVVZ was sliced away by the Gestapo during 1940. More and more loyal Czechs learned of the midnight knock on the door. It was a sound which almost none of those who responded to it would hear a second time.

Unlike their counterparts in France or Yugoslavia which waxed ever stronger under British, then American, forced-feeding, the resistance "fraternities" in Czechoslovakia were mercilessly crushed. Soon, there was scanty surviving memory to attest to their ephemeral existence.

Milada was among the last to be snatched up by the Nazis. She made use of her valuable contacts at City Hall and in Parliament, now the precincts of the Nazis and their collaborators, to obtain hints of German intentions both in the Balkans and beyond. There was a rumor, but obviously a wild one, that Hitler was preparing a Sunday punch to stagger the Russians. It was not, however, unthinkable to Milada. She knew from previous experience with both the Germans and the Russians that there was no especial honor between these two well-experienced thieves.

Milada, unfortunately, never had a chance to capitalize on the channels she was opening. The enemy was becoming all too aware of how well informed she was.

She and her husband, Bohuslav, were resting briefly on August 2 in a small hotel in the beautiful Bohemian-Moravian highlands. Since both their place of lodging and its town, Horni Bradle, were obscure, even to many Czechs, it was obvious that an informer had led the secret police to their room.

Milada was considered the more dangerous of the pair because of her work in PVVZ and in the Council of Czechoslovak Women, itself a natural rallying point for opposition. She was taken to the Petchek Palace in Prague, which had been commandeered by Himmler's police, then placed in a small cell resembling a chimney. In it she could only stand. When she sagged from weariness a guard would open a small iron door in the bricking and dash cold water in her face.

After successive days of starvation, she successfully imitated faintings. Stürmbahnführer Pfitch, the massive, one-eyed prison commandant, ordered that her hands be pricked with needles and her feet singed with tapers. Since wincing is an involuntary reflex, she could not continue to fool the guards. Angered, they chained her to walls, even as Violette Szabo had been, and abandoned her for hours at a time.

Presently, she was removed to the infamous "Jewish cell" in Pankrac Prison where her eyeglasses were removed and smashed into fragments on the floor. They switched her with fagots. They awakened her in the middle of the night with bright lights. In fact, they did everything but kill Milada.

Her wounds became infected from the chains and her many trouncings. In mounting frustration, the Germans transferred her to the still more formidable stone jail on King Charles Square—Karlovo Prison. Changing their methods, her captors placed Milada in cells with sick prostitutes, hoping that she would be revolted into telling them anything, just so that she could be removed from the foul place. They did not know their prisoner very well.

Now Milada was shunted to Terezin "fortress" prison, distinct from the infamous ghetto of the same name. It had, nonetheless, earned its own black reputation, ranking as only a slightly junior Natzweiler, Dachau, and Auschwitz.

Here she took her jailors by surprise. In marked contempt to her silence, she "talked," but only as Louise de Bettignies once had confused her own interrogators with a hodgepodge of misinformation and partial truths.

Nonetheless, her game playing would consume many months before the Nazis came to the conclusion that they had been shamelessly hoodwinked. During this breathing space, Milada was placed in charge of the prison hospital, so called, since there was no surgeon or even a nurse in attendance. She not only took care of her less strong fellow prisoners as best she could, but shared her food. She employed at the same time her greater freedom to obtain messengers—loyal Czech employees at Terezin—who would convey news of their loved ones to the families of prisoners.

"We began to receive secret news about her proud, even rebellious attitude," recalled Arnost Heidrich, a colleague and authority in international law, who had escaped imprisonment, "toward her Nazi jailors. I can imagine what a beneficent influence this proud attitude of a Czech woman must have had on the minds of those who suffered with her from the Nazi barbarism."

Terezin's angel of mercy was nearly exhausted. Not only was her "telegraph" system discovered and her charades during interrogation, but as well an event wholly beyond her control had superheated the fury of the enemy.

Reinhard ("The Hangman") Heydrich, Himmler's blond, youthful top lieutenant—the "home office" man outranking the only relatively more queasy Henlein—had been assassinated. In reprisal, his successor, tall, gray, hawk-nosed Karl Hermann Frank, formerly a Sudeten deputy to Henlein, had ordered the total eradication of Lidice. This former mining village about twenty miles west of Prague was supposedly the rendezvous for some of the assassins.

All of its citizens were shot or deported. Only one of the more than two hundred males of Lidice lived to tell of the horror that would make its very name a symbol of bestiality. The town was burned, then its scorched ruins dynamited, and finally the rubble bulldozed into the earth—far more efficiently destroyed than Carthage.

A lust for revenge extended throughout the unhappy land, especially into prisons, always a tempting reservoir for the Nazis' sacrificial lambs. Among this tragic number was Frantiska Plaminkova. Milada met her just briefly in Terezin—or perhaps only caught a fleeting glimpse of her in the dungeonlike corridors—on her way to the guillotine. This form of execution, peculiarly medieval, had been revived in Germany after the Nazis came to power.

"Protector" of Bohemia and Moravia, Frank apparently was in accord with his Berlin masters on this and all other matters. So was Emil Hacha, still Czechoslovakia's nominal President, who had gone so far as to send a message of condolence to Heydrich's next of kin.

Somehow, Milada escaped Mme. Plaminkova's fate. However, Director Jockl, of Terezin, ordered her placed in the prison's deepest dungeons—black, dank, with eight-foot-thick walls of brick and stone. When Jockl believed she was "cooperating," he had gone so far as to order a new pair of glasses. Now, once more they were snatched from her face and stamped into the stone floors.

Word by this time had filtered down, remarkably, that Milada was a secretary of President Benes, who was now heading Czechoslovakia's government-in-exile from London. This belief increased her bad treatment—"thirty-six separated investigations" was her own count of her pummelings.

Others had broken under torture and told everything they knew, and probably more that they really did not know. It did them little good. Of forty-three key men of "Verni Zustaneme," thirty-two had already been shot, hung, strangled, beheaded, or died from unconscionable mistreatment, like dogs.

Thin, gray, her skin brittle, Milada was at long last removed from Terezin to Germany—for trial. Even to face a court was something of an honor in the Nazis' twisted sense of jurisprudence and logic. A signed death warrant was sufficient—but the Nazis were meticulous that there always be a warrant, and someone to sign it.

"She left the dungeon," recalled Dr. Horak, who now lives in exile in Washington, D.C. (in conversations with me), "only when the time of her trial approached. That was in the summer of 1944. Until October, 1944, she was then in the prisons of Leipzig and Dresden. I was at that time imprisoned in Golnow, near Stettin, and we met again only at the trial.

"The trial took place at the end of October, 1944, in the Dresden prison, 'Anstalt I.' To the court she brought me a present, some pieces of bread, which she economized from her own portion in the prison. The public prosecutor proposed the death penalty for her.

"It was a terribly hard moment. But the court, after deliberating, sentenced her to eight years in prison, and me for five years. Later, the Gestapo, not satisfied with the sentence, asked for a new trial, but the proposal came too late. The war was almost over.

"Many good friends were executed in the meantime. They all accepted their sentence with courage. The Jews in our group were not tried. They were returned to the Gestapo to be disposed of otherwise, without trial and, as I heard, they were executed later somewhere near Berlin."

Milada was sent to a woman's prison at Aichach, twenty-five miles northwest of Dachau. Her husband went to Ebern, in Bavaria. Even in prison, Milada heard talk from the Communist women confined with her of the "takeover" once Germany was defeated. As a matter of fact, American POW's had experienced their own difficulties with arrogant Russian captives who persistently refused to cooperate in Stalag or camp affairs even though it meant their own physical betterment. "Nyet" early had become a word symbolic of the whole Russian attitude, or lack of attitude.

Compared to prior incarcerations and torture, Aichach was a convalescent home. Her old routine by which Milada "started every day with a prayer and good exercise," as she mentioned later, was uninterrupted the last six months of her confinement.

Liberated by General Patton's onrushing armored juggernaut, Milada arrived back in Prague on May 20, two days before her husband. The capital at least had been spared the destruction of war. The couple was able to find another flat in the same Smichov section where they had lived previously.

Friends remarked on Milada's "fresh and healthy" appearance in spite of nearly five years in prison. She seemed as strong and vital as the day she had been arrested at the little hotel in the highlands.

Back in her beloved home city, which she referred to as a "pearl," she returned to an approximation of the life and career she had known before the war. She hoped that, somehow, the republic could be reborn. And it was—for a little while.

The villains of yesterday all at once seemed so implausible that they might not have existed at all. Karl Frank was hung in Prague's Pankrac Prison while three thousand Czechs, including six heavily veiled widows of Lidice, watched impassively.

Slightly more than a month later, on June 30, Emil Hacha died while awaiting trial. The enormity of his own crimes seemed to have weighed on his conscience, since in his final days of captivity he had appeared to have forgotten his own name.

There was still much human flotsam left in the wake of those villains. Trying to do something about it, Milada organized an Association of Political Prisoners and Survivors of the Victims of Nazism. There were so many widows and young children as well as orphans . . .

Dr. Benes, back in office at historic Hradcany Castle, personally awarded Milada a military decoration and the First Class Merit Medal for both her resistance activities and her postwar efforts.

She projected herself into the rebuilding of her country with the highest idealism, soon assuming leadership of the Women's Council, left adrift by what amounted to the murder of Senator Plaminkova. Milada was also elected to Parliament as a member of the National Socialist party, a party which had already proven an especial target for Communist venom.

The survivor of the worst of Nazi tortures had good reason to question whether villainy could be contemplated in the past tense. In fact, she was among the first, and not necessarily excepting Benes himself, to recognize that the Czechoslovakia Communist party was about as altruistic as the Sudetenland Nazis. It was working on orders from Moscow to convert the nation into another Soviet satellite.

This became especially apparent to her during a tour of

the USSR capital arranged for European women leaders. It was no coincidence that her roommate was Anezka Hodinova Spurna, a Communist congresswoman from Prague. Obviously enough, Mlle. Spurna alternated a silent surveillance of her countrywoman with crude and wholly unconvincing appeals to Milada to swing over to the Communist party. Such interest might have proven flattering to some.

"Moscow," her husband later observed, perhaps wryly, "had a negative effect upon her."

Milada united seventy-eight women's organizations, departments, and committees under one parent: the Czechoslovak Women's Council—but in vain. This huge and influential assemblage was itself infiltrated by the Reds. Loyal members were intimidated until they either resigned, to be replaced by hard-core Soviet sympathizers, or refused in their frightened apathy to take a stand on anything—even, absurd and unlikely as it seemed, on the question of a woman's right to work.

As her old associate and former Lord Mayor of Prague, Dr. Petr Zenkl, recalled, the women's group "became a battlefield, rather than a field of cooperation. The prisoners' association which she formed was also subverted by the Communists.

"Thus Dr. Horakova's work in all the fields of her activity changed to a fight against the growing terror of the Communists. In her electoral district she saw with great anxiety a representative of her own political party adapt himself to the Communists and succumb to their influence. She openly attacked him and asked him to answer directly her question about his attitude toward the Communists."

A "national disaster," predicted Zenkl (who, like Horak, now lives in Washington), was "in the making."

Arnost Heidrich, her old lawyer friend, recalled her mounting concerns.

"If the Kremlin is not satisfied with the knowledge that our people have always behaved friendly toward Russia notwithstanding the regime they had," she confided to him, "it clearly signified that Stalin, just like Hitler, is more interested in the limitation of the power of the Czechoslovak state and enslavement of the Czechoslovak people than in friendship and alliance with the Czechoslovak Republic.

"That must be resisted from the beginning. We must build in time a counterweight against Stalin's designs against Czechoslovakia by enlarging and strengthening our friendly relations with the West."

This she was able to do through her work as Women's Council leader and as a member of Parliament's Foreign Policy Committee. She met emissaries of the West in other capitals and discussed with them the plight of the little republic. She sought to establish her own channels of communication. Milada believed, as she had discussed with Heidrich, that there was time to save Czechoslovakia.

But there was not. The amoebae of totalitarianism were already multiplying with the speed of light.

The "national disaster" augured by Zenkl hit on February 25, 1948, when Klement Gottwald, long-time agitator and Premier since 1946, confronted Dr. Benes at Hradcany Castle. The short, paunchy Stalinist presented the President with his list of twenty-two new cabinet ministers for rubber stamping. All were either Communist, Socialist, or "safe."

"You're talking to me like Hitler!" Benes protested.

Gottwald was acting in character. In 1929, when he snatched his first seat in Parliament, this rather colorless Bolshevist, with the sharply unpleasant features, had snapped, "you gentlemen are asking me what we are here for. My answer is simple—we are here to break your necks and I promise you most solemnly we will do it."

Immensely impatient, Gottwald strode from his chair, which, like everything else in the castle, was a museum piece, and stood before one of the ceiling-high leaded windows. Then, with a dramatic gesture of pounding his fists together he turned and warned of revolt.

"Look!" he said. "The crowds in the street. You can see them, and hear them. You would not be able to walk through Wenceslaus Square!"

Gottwald's cruelty was his trademark. Friend and foe alike used to parrot the bitter jest, "He would kill his own mother," then at once contradicting with mock seriousness, "No, that is not possible. He already has."

Perhaps Benes had no more choice than Chamberlain or Daladier had at Munich a decade earlier. Whether he had or not, he signed. The "coup" was legalized.

Within hours the frontiers were closed. Cold terror once again within a short lifetime seized the people of Czechoslovakia. Some attempted escape, a few—with no heart to go through *it* all over again—shot themselves, swallowed poison, or jumped from windows or bridges. One government official whose neck had been figuratively broken by Gottwald, Dr. Prokop Drtina, tried but failed.

The great purge spread like a cancer even into quarters which to the non-communist world appeared palpably absurd—to the composition, for example, of soccer and tennis teams.

Democracy in Czechoslavakia was dying "without a whimper," by default. None, certainly not those who had helped in its creation, seemed to care sufficiently to endeavor to resuscitate the near-corpse, almost as moribund as the Roman Empire.

Milada pleaded with Jozka David, the President of Parliament, to convoke its members to fight aggressively against the Communists. He would not. She called on Jan Masaryk, foreign minister and son of the late President, who had become a virtual prisoner in the Czernin Palace, guarded by twenty-three secret policemen. Microphones were secreted throughout his apartment. He had been the recipient of bombs (which failed to go off) mailed to him. Any visitor risked his or her life merely to be observed entering Masaryk's apartment.

"I will do it," he asserted obliquely to her. Milada assumed he meant he would try to escape across the border.

The statesman may have had something else on his mind. A few days following Milada's visit, on March 10, the sixty-one-year-old Czech patriot was found dead on the paving beneath the opened window of his third-story apartment.

Milada, hearing of the tragedy minutes after its occurring, raced to the Czernin Palace to view Masaryk's sheet-covered body. Afterward, she alluded only to his "badly smashed heels."

He was "depressed," asserted *Rude Pravo* the Communist newspaper. He had "jumped." Or—had he, really?

Within hours Milada resigned from Parliament. She was dissuaded by her friends from making a speech attacking the Communist "outrage." Already, they reminded her, she was in jeopardy because of her outspoken views, specifically in recent months for her paper against farm collectivization, "Facing the Village."

Dr. Zenkl and other patriots were already under house arrest. Milada visited them with the same boldness she had manifested in seeing Masaryk. Dr. Drtina, recovering, asserted he had attempted to take his own life in protest against Benes' "surrender" to Gottwald.

"I tried to persuade her to escape before it was too late," Zenkl said. "I still can see her . . . how she jumped up and repeated with shining eyes full of courage and self-confidence Masaryk's famous words: 'Jesus not Caesar.' Then she said: " 'Here at home is my place, and here I will work as long as possible. There are many others abroad who are more capable than I am, and I am needed here, at home. Nothing else seems important today, only our task. One who had been for such a long time in Nazi concentration camps as I had, and had been condemned to death by the Germans, became free of all fear of anything that a man could do to another. And I do not believe my countrymen can be worse than the Germans.' "

But some of them were, some like Gottwald. Mindful of Stalin's starving to death in the 1930's of six million dissident Kulaks, or peasants, the Czechoslovak dictator created accumulating obstacles to the continuing livelihoods of those who in any way threatened his despotism. "Certificates of reliability" were a prerequisite to employment.

Decrees were published in ever lengthening columns daily in *Rude Pravo* noting the dismissal from office of state figures, both important and less important. Milada herself was "expelled" from a number of organizations with which she had never even been affiliated.

Wasn't there something, even some little thing, that Dr. Benes could do? Could he not speak, if but a few whispered words to remind the world of the Czechoslovakia that used to be? Milada implored him to do so.

In his consuming weariness of spirit he urged her "not to

worry." He would, if necessary, "appeal to the army." In any event, he was sure that Catholicism must sooner or later manifest itself as a "natural barrier to communism."

He forgot, or preferred not to remind himself, that the army had become Gottwald's army, and backing up that army was a yet greater one: the USSR divisions, as many as needed, spearheaded by heavy tanks.

Desperately searching here and there for someone, anyone who could suggest a way to buy just a little more time for Czechoslovakia, she visited Heidrich. He had become rather a father confessor to her.

"Milada," he wrote (for this book), "unexpectedly opened the door of my office in Czernin Palace. I surmised why she was coming and I realized that she did not know about the 'bugging' of my office by the Communists. Therefore I gave her a sign not to speak, or to speak only of nonpolitical matters.

"The same evening my confidence man explained to her the situation, and asked her to see me at my home. He told her that I must be very careful in relations with my friends, and that even my house was being watched, and asked her to come to see me only after dusk."

Becoming more and more enmeshed in the feeble existing opposition to communism, Milada paid Heidrich regular visits, up until the hour of his own escape. She had become sort of a secret agent extraordinary, a last dynamic and effective patriot in the wake of a country that no one, no one seemingly but herself, minded being buried.

"I witnessed," Heidrich continued, "Her cooperation in the foundation of our third resistance movement abroad. She tried to prepare escape for some of our politicians who by their importance and experience were predestined for the work in the resistance movement abroad.

"I also witnessed her careful effort to facilitate the lives of those who were under police control. But especially I witnessed Milada's organization of our domestic resistance.

"She was not only its initiator but its moving spirit and motor force. Her unparalleled courage, manyfold resourcefulness, and working energy were unlimited.

"Armed with the experience in the anti-Nazi resistance movement abroad, a perfect and reliable domestic organization must be founded. This organization must then provide the systematic information to execute the orders of the resistance movement abroad."

Milada pursued her own perilous course—one woman attempting to save a republic, or else find some way to pump strength and vitality back into it. To the cynical Communists such a Lilliputian spectacle should have seemed wholly ludicrous.

A realist at the same time, she was not confident of what might be expected from the preoccupied West. Only the Soviet Union in 1948 seemed to possess the stomach and desire for further conflict. Milada was "depressed by the weak reaction of Western Great Powers."

In June, Dr. Benes dropped all pretense of office. He submitted his formal resignation to Gottwald, who at once assumed the Presidency with the spontaneity of a fox lunging at a fat chicken. Three months later, Benes, an unhappy, tragic figure, was dead.

Klement Gottwald not only arranged a showy state funeral but was the principal and most solemn mourner. Most surely, as the last muffled drum roll was swallowed in the Gothic majesty of the old city, the republic was relegated to memory and the back shelves of history.

Milada's husband was in a compromising position. He barely held onto his old job at the Ministry of Information.

Not of quite the same emotional caliber as his wife, although he wholly believed in the cause for which she fought, he nonetheless did not see the present issues as ones which could be resolved other than in the course of long years' time. He also was aware of the demands and needs of a teen-age daughter.

Bohuslav, although he possessed no passport, saw escape as the only immediate solution to his own problem and the problem of many others like him. Dr. Zenkl, Rose Pelantova, and others, also without passports, had, one by one, slipped out of Prague during late 1948 and 1949—to turn up in the West. Paradoxically, in the changing kaleidoscope of war and war's aftermath, West Germany, under Allied military control, had become a highly desirable haven. The town of Hof, northwest of Munich, and a base for the US Army armored corps, was but a sprint from the westernmost bulge of Czechoslovakia.

"Many people," Milada's husband recalled, "passed through our apartment, and the information they brought was smuggled abroad. We both knew that such an activity must stop one day, and that we must escape in time. We decided that Milada would go first, and I would follow with our daughter.

"There were many ways to escape, and many were still open, but the apparent lack of danger seemed to make the escape unnecessary. We discussed the problems of our escape often, and we were absolutely sure that there was no other way left for us, only the escape.

"My participation in her work was rather modest. I was not a member of her group, and I practically performed only some subsidiary services. The most important of these was perhaps the preparation of the gathered information for the way abroad.

"I, of course, knew the members of her group, and I was surprised to read only the names of some of them, and many other names of persons who were not members of her group, among the [subsequent] defendants.

"I never attended the meetings of the group. I know only that one of the meetings, and a very risky one, took place in Vinor and that Milada returned from the meeting very excited. What happened at the meeting, I do not know.

"Perhaps in connection with this meeting, I proposed to Milada to go abroad together, all three of us. She almost agreed to leave at once, but later changed her mind and stayed in Czechoslovakia. Soon afterward, I was sent on a paid vacation, and was not allowed to return to my office.

"The situation was ripe for escape, I really do not know why we hesitated to go.

"The tension grew fast. Repeatedly I asked Milada if the people with whom she had been working have a reliable confidence man at the police station, who would warn us in time, if somebody were arrested. She did not give me a direct answer, but I had the impression that such a confidence man existed.

"Early in the summer of 1949, one of the members of her group, Dr. Vaclav Sykora, suddenly disappeared. He used to be President Benes' secretary, a man whom Dr. Benes trusted; therefore we all had complete confidence in him. His disappearance raised all kinds of suppositions. Finally we discovered that he had been arrested by the Communists.

"On September 27, 1949, early in the morning, I accompanied Milada downtown. She went to her office, and I tried to get some necessary information. She wanted me to return home at noon, because of our daughter Jana, and I promised to do it.

"The day was nice and very clear, an Indian summer day in Prague, and on that day I talked to Milada for the last time. We separated in the lower part of the Wenceslaus Square, and I never saw her again.

"In the afternoon I was sitting on the terrace of our house, when, suddenly, two men in dirty raincoats rang the bell.

"Our housekeeper let them in. They were secret police agents. They placed me, Jana, and the housekeeper in the various rooms of the apartment and waited for more policemen who were supposed to search the apartment.

"I knew that Milada planned to attend in the afternoon a meeting in Dr. Jina's house. So, trying to get away and warn her, I somehow quite miraculously escaped. I discovered that she was not yet in Dr. Jina's apartment. I arranged it so that they would notify me immediately of her arrival.

"But for all that, it was too late. She had been arrested in her office in Masna ulice, at three P.M. I learned about it only the next day. Not able to help her and afraid that I might aggravate her case, if arrested, I kept hiding for two months and finally escaped across the border on December 1, 1949."

Milada had every reason to expect treatment the same as she received at the hands of the Gestapo. She was not, as a matter of fact, tortured physically. But she was interrogated sometimes as long as sixty hours without interruption.

Rude Pravo described her as a "bandit," an "enemy of the workers," one who had caused the "peoples' outrage." These sort of diatribes had long appeared in the Soviet press, and they usually were preludes to "show" trials and predetermined verdicts. The accused were invariably "guilty," and the punishment just as certainly "death"!

"*Todestraffe!*" was the way the Germans put it, and the

very word rolled with the sound of a firing squad.

But the Communists waited until spring—spring when the soft pink roses were blooming once more in Petrin Park and young lovers again sat holding hands on the banks of the Dvina and listened to the carillons of Our Lady of Loreto. The Communists waited not because they could not bring themselves to try Milada, but for the reason that they still wished her to "confess," and one day, perhaps, agree to work for them. Gottwald himself, from long professional acquaintance, was aware of Milada's unusual abilities in several fields. Nor had he any compunctions against putting his sworn enemies to work for him, if he could maneuver it.

Finally her "crime," and that of three other rather obscure male co-defendants, was published in *Rude Pravo:* she had "tried to undermine the people's democratic system of government."

The *people,* however, had not been consulted. The people of Prague and of Czechoslovakia were the people whose children Milada Horakova had helped in so many ways; the people were men and women whose right to vote she had endeavored to secure for all time; the people were those whom, in times of hunger, she had helped to feed and, in sorrow, to comfort.

The *people* would not place Milada on trial. The Communists, through their figurehead, Klement Gottwald, would— and did.

In defiance Milada faced her accusers. The trial was broadcast—for the world, if it was interested, to hear. In West German immigration camps, many who had fled Czechoslovakia sat by their radio sets, among them Milada's husband and daughter.

She spoke at great length, words that could well be in the

preamble to a bill of rights for a new Czechoslovakia should the republic ever be reborn:

"We are standing here firm and unshaken," she concluded, "expecting the strongest sentence. In this most difficult hour we are strengthened by the knowledge that we are not alone in our action, that after our departure our effort will not end.

"Abroad in the free world, there are men who will continue our fight and who will prove that ours was a just cause. . . ."

The "strongest sentence" was pronounced, one even the Nazis never dared pass.

Protests poured in from the world over, signed by a distinguished list of personages led by Mrs. Eleanor Roosevelt, and organizations of such prominence as committees of the United Nations. Statesmen, educators, a former president of Norway, artists, authors, and religious leaders, all joined in a plea for clemency.

But Gottwald knew no mercy. Milada and the other three accused were hung in Pankrac Prison in June, 1950, while international cables were still tapping their entreaties and mute sense of horror into Prague.

Milada died a martyr beyond question, in the same city where John Huss, the religious reformer, was burned at the stake exactly 535 years previously. He had made the grave error of defying authority—in this ancient case, the power of Emperor Sigismund of the Holy Roman Empire and of His Holiness Pope Alexander V. These two potentates possessed roughly the same sort of relationship as respectively Gottwald did to Stalin. Unquestionably, there were other similarities.

(The two Communists, one large, the other very small,

would themselves die within nine days of each other. Klement Gottwald succumbed to what was announced as pneumonia on March 14, 1953, after attending the funeral of Premier Stalin in Moscow. The Czechoslovakian dictator's own score for murder had been on an uninterrupted increase. In the last four months of his life he had kicked nine government leaders to the gallows, led by his lifelong "friend" and secretary general of the Czech Communist Party, Rudolf Slansky.)

Those who believe in the democratic form of government can ponder only with shame why one woman, not physically very imposing at all, was almost the only one who fought to her death to save a whole nation? Why had she never fallen prey to a frustration which had seized others?

With her passing, the world became infinitely poorer. Her violent death bequeathed an almost impossible heritage. Who was worthy of it?

None who knew or worked with her think of Milada as truly dead. Her husband puts it this way: "Milada remains for me on the stage of life."

Jan Dzban, a fellow resistance worker, notes in more dimension: "She was able to prove something that nations, states, and collective groups in general never could prove, namely that sometimes individuals can tower above the masses, putting concern about their own safety somewhere in a remote and hidden corner of their consciousness . . . silently, conscious of the danger, when death was coldly covering the whole horizon, she refused to take refuge in a set of poor moral values. In those moments, meekly bowed knees and a bent head would not have marred her heroic picture but she held her head high, her knees did not bend, and her heart overcame reason.

". . . she proved overwhelmingly what was the real and purest meaning of the word courage. She shook from it the accumulated dust and litter. It makes one pause and think, and feel better, and the feeling warms your heart, because it proves that the world is not as bad as it seems, that it just cannot be completely rotten. Do you doubt it?

"Do not despair, we do not live in litter and ashes, because we all lived in the world of Milada Horakova."

On the stage of life yet, as her husband thinks of her? Perhaps.

But what of the greater, gentler, freer world which was her long dream? Was her sacrifice in vain? Can the ever darkening clouds be rolled back to reveal the dawn that Milada must have glimpsed?

The Communists, with their childlike propensity for changing history to fit their own twisted canvases, sought to erase Milada Horakova wholly from the chronicle of Prague in this century, and of the Czechoslovak state. Not a mention is made in contemporary Czech publications of her, either in her resistance to the Nazis or in her great contributions to social welfare, especially in the children's field.

But again, the Communists are closing only their own eyes. They cannot pretend that this woman never lived, no matter how strongly they will it, or legislate that desire.

What she meant will indeed, as her husband said, remain on "the stage of life." Her image persists to confront us, to challenge us, to shame us in the West—the image of Milada Horakova, the woman on our conscience.

BIBLIOGRAPHY

Adams, George W. *Doctors in Blue*, Henry Schuman, New York, 1952.

Anderson, T. S. *The Command of the Howe Brothers During the Revolution*, Oxford University Press, New York, 1936.

Army Times Editors. *The Tangled Web*, Robert Luce Inc., Washington, 1963.

Aston, Sir George. *Secret Service*, Faber & Faber, London, 1930.

Babington-Smith, Constance. *Air Spy*, Harper & Brothers, New York, 1957.

Bakeless, John. *Turncoats, Traitors and Heroes*, J. B. Lippincott & Co., Philadelphia, 1959.

Balde, Jean. *Jeune Filles de France*, Editions Spes, Paris, 1937.

Barton, George. *The World's Greatest Military Spies*, Page Co., Boston, 1917.

Binder, Henri. *Espionage et Contre-Espionage A Bruxelles, 1914–18*, Payot, Paris, 1935.

Bleicher, Henri. *Colonel Henri's Story*, Kimber, Ltd., London, 1954.

Boudinot, Elias. *Journal, or Historical Recollections of American Events During the Revolutionary War*, Frederick, Philadelphia, 1894.

Boyd, Belle. *In Camp and Prison*, Saunders, Otley & Co., London, 1865.

Buckmaster, Col. Maurice. *They Fought Alone*, Odhams, London, 1958.

Churchill, Peter. *Duel of Wits*, G. P. Putnam's Sons, New York, 1955.

Collier, Basil. *The Battle of The V-Weapons*, Hodder & Stoughton, London, 1964.

Cookridge, Edward H. *Secrets of the British Secret Service*, Sampson Low, London, 1948.

———. *Sisters of Delilah*, Oldbourne, London, 1959.

Coulson, Major Thomas. *The Queen of Spies*, Constable & Co., London, 1935.

d'Argoeuves, Helene. *Louise de Bettignies*, Vieux Colombier, Paris, 1956.

de Gramont, Sanche. *The Secret War*, G. P. Putnam's Sons, New York, 1962.

de Jong, Louis. *The German Fifth Column in The Second World War*, Routledge & Kegan Paul, London, 1956.

Duke, Basil. *A History of Morgan's Cavalry*, Indiana University Press, Bloomington, 1960.

Duke, Madelaine. *Top Secret Mission*, Pan Books, London, 1957.

"E-7." *Women Spies I Have Known*, Hurst & Blackett, London, 1939.

Everitt, Nicholas. *British Secret Service During the Great War*, Hutchinson, London, 1920.

Felix, Christopher. *The Spy and His Masters*, Secker & Warburg, London, 1963.

Firmin, Stanley. *They Came to Spy*, Hutchinson, London, 1947.

Fiske, John. *The American Revolution*, Houghton Mifflin & Co., Boston, 1891.

Foot, Michael R. D. *S.O.E. in France*, Her Majesty's Stationary Office, London, 1966.

Foote, Alexander. *Handbook for Spies*, Museum Press, London, 1964.

Fuller, Jean Overton. *The Starr Affair*, Victor Gollancz, London, 1952.

Goemaere, Pierre. *Histoire de la Libre Belgique*, Bureau de la Libre Belgique, Brussels, 1919.

Grant, Hamil. *Spies and Secret Service*, Frederick A. Stokes, New York, 1915.

Greenhow, Mrs. Rose O'Neal. *My Imprisonment*, Bentley, London, 1863.

Hall, Oliver (translator for Antoine Redier). *The Story of Louise de Bettignies*, Hutchinson Ltd., London, 1926.

Hoehling, A. A. *A Whisper of Eternity* (The Story of Edith Cavell), Thomas Yoseloff, New York, 1957.

Hoehling, Mary. *Girl Soldier and Spy*, Julian Messner, New York, 1959.

Holland, Cecil F. *Morgan and His Raiders*, The Macmillan Co., New York, 1942.

Horan, James D. *Desperate Women*, G. P. Putnam's Sons, New York, 1952.

Howarth, Patrick. *Special Operations*, Routledge & Kegan Paul, London, 1955.

Jones, Katharine M. *Heroines of Dixie*, Bobbs Merrill Co., New York, 1955.

Jowitt, William. *Some Were Spies*, Hodder & Stoughton, London, 1954.

Koeves, Tibor. *Satan in Top Hat*, Alliance Book Corp., New York, 1941.

Landau, Capt. Henry. *The Enemy Within*, G. P. Putnam's Sons, New York, 1937.

———. *Secrets of the White Lady*, G. P. Putnam's Sons, New York, 1935.

Lossing, Benson J. *The Pictorial Field Book of The Revolution*, Harper and Brothers, New York, 1852.

MacDonald, E. P. *Undercover Girl*, The Macmillan Co., New York, 1947.

Many, Martin. *Quatre Ans Aves Les Barbares*, Renaissance du Livre, Paris, 1919.

Marshall, Bruce. *The White Rabbit*, Houghton Mifflin Co., Boston, 1952.

Martinelli, George. *The Man Who Saved London*, Doubleday & Co., New York, 1961.

Michigan Volunteers in the Civil War. Ihling Bros., Kalamazoo, 1905.

Millis, Walter. *Road to War*, Houghton Mifflin Co., Boston, 1935.

Minney, E. J. *Carve Her Name With Pride*, Newnes, London, 1956.

Moriaud, Gem. *Louise de Bettignies*, Editions Jules Tallander, Paris, 1928.

Newman, Bernard. *Epics of Espionage*, Philosophical Library, New York, 1951.

———. *The World of Espionage*, Souvenir Press, London, 1962.

Nicholas, Elizabeth. *Death Be Not Proud*, Cresset Press, London, 1958.

Nicolai, Col. Walther. *The German Secret Service*, Stanley Paul & Co., Ltd., London, 1924.

Perles, Alfred. *Great True Spy Adventures*, Arco Publishers, London, 1957.

Power, James R. *Brave Women and Their Wartime Decorations*, Vantage Press, New York, 1959.

Read, Conyers. *Mr. Secretary Walsingham*, Oxford University Press, London, 1925.

Ross, Ishbel. *Rebel Rose*, Harper and Brothers, New York, 1954.

Rowan, Richard Wilmer. *The Story of the Secret Service*, John Miles, Ltd., London, 1938.

Sarmiento, Ferdinand L. *Life of Pauline Cushman*, John Lovell Co., New York, 1865.

Scott, Samuel W. *History of the Thirteenth Regiment Tennessee Volunteer Cavalry*, Ziegler & Co., Philadelphia, 1903.

Senour, The Rev. F. *Morgan and His Captors*, C. F. Vent & Co., Cincinnati, 1865.

Singer, Kurt. *Spies and Traitors of World War II*, Prentice Hall, New York, 1945.

——. *The World's Greatest Spies*, W. H. Allen, London, 1951.

——. *The World's Thirty Greatest Women Spies*, Wilfrid Funk, New York, 1951.

Swiggett, Howard. *The Rebel Raider*, Bobbs Merrill Co., Indianapolis, 1934.

Tallmadge, Benjamin. *Memoirs*, Thomas Holman, New York, 1858.

Thuliez, Louise. *Condemned to Death*, Methuen, London, 1934.

Tickell, Jerrard. *Odette*, Chapman and Hall, London, 1949.

Turrou, Leon. *The Nazi Spy Conspiracy in America*, Random House, New York, 1939.

von Bernstorff, Count Johann. *Memoirs*, Random House, New York, 1936.

von Papen, Franz. *Memoirs of Franz von Papen*, Andre Deutsch, London, 1952.

Voska, Emanuel V. *Spy and Counter-Spy*, Doubleday Doran, New York, 1940.

Ward, Dame Irene. *F.A.N.Y. Invicta*, Hutchinson, London, 1955.

Webb, Anthony. *The Natzweiler Trial*, William Hodge & Co., Ltd., London, 1949.

Wescott, Thompson. *The Historic Mansions and Buildings of Philadelphia*, Porter and Coates, Philadelphia, 1877.

Whitehead, Don. *The FBI Story*, Random House, New York, 1956.
Writings of George Washington. U.S. Government Printing Office, Washington, D.C., 1933.
Yardley, Herbert O. *The American Black Chamber*, Bobbs Merrill Co., Indianapolis, 1931.
Young, Agathe. *The Women and the Crisis*, McDowell, Obolensky, New York, 1959.

INDEX

Alexander V, Pope, 190
Alice Service, 53-69
"Ambroise," 122
American Revolution, 3-17
Anastasie, 120-121
"Archambaud," (Gilbert Norman), 124, 132
Armistice Commission, 72
Arnold, Gen. Benedict, 16

Babbington-Smith, Constance, 156
Bacon, Orville, 41
Bacon, Orville, Jr., 43
Bacon, Sarah, see Thompson, Sarah
Baissac, Lise de, 139-141
Baseden, Yvonne, 138-139
Bates, Ann, 4n.
Baucq, Philippe, 65
Beekman, Yolande, 131-132, 134
Behrens, Theresa, 110
Belle Boyd in Camp and Prison (Boyd), 20
Benes, Edouard, 169, 170, 175, 178, 180, 181, 183, 185, 187
Bergensfjord (ship), 87
Bernstorff, Count Johann Friedrich von, 78, 83
Bettignies, Henri de, 46, 47
Bettignies, Henri de, Jr., 48, 49

Bettignies, Louise Marie Jeanne Henriette de, 46-73
Bettignies, Mabille de, 47, 73
Beville, Baron de, 93
Bissing, Baron Moritz von, 65
Bleicher, Sgt. Hugo, 133-134
Bloch, Denise, 122, 139
Blucher, Elizabeth, 101
Blucher, Oswald, 111
Blucher, Otto, 101
Blucher, Velvalee Malvena, see Dickinson, Velvalee
Bonnefois, Kitty, 141
Bopp, Franz, 81
Borrel, Andrée, 124, 128, 139
Boudinot, Col. Elias, 5-6, 11-13
Boy-Ed, Capt. Karl, 78-80
Boyd, Belle, 19-21, 22, 23, 24
Bragg, Gen. Braxton, 25
Briscoe, Norah Lavinia, 150
Brooks, Lt. Edward J., 36, 42, 43
Brownlow, Col. John S., 36, 42
Bryan, William Jennings, 88
Buchanan-Dineen, Grace, 110-111
Buckmaster, Maurice, 132
Bull Run, battle of, 21
Bulmer, Robert, 157
Bultzingsloven, Bruno von, 81
Burgoyne, Gen. John, 4, 16

Burnside, Gen. Ambrose, 31
Bushell, Charles, 118
Byck, Muriel, 133

Cadwalader, Capt. John, 7
Campbell, Andrew, 38-39
Carter, Gen. S. G., 43
Cavell, Edith, 64-69, 132, 167
"Celine," see Sansom, Odette Marie
Chamberlain, Neville, 168, 170, 181
"Charlotte" (Marie Leonie van
    Houtte), 53, 64, 65, 68, 71, 73
Church, William, 147
Churchill, Capt. Peter Morland, 133-
    136, 142
Churchill, Winston, 117, 142, 155,
    162
Civil War, 18-44
Clark, Maj. John, Jr., 6, 10, 13
Clinton, Sir Henry, 16
Cornioley, Henri, 138
Condor (ship), 23
Cotten, James W., 43
Cotten, Sarah, see Thompson, Sarah
Coulson, Pierre, 62-63
Craig, Lt. Col. Thomas, 11
Croy, Princess Marie de, 64
Cushman, "Maj." Pauline, 25-26, 27

Damerment, Charles, 130
Damerment, Madeleine, 130-132, 134
Darragh, Lt. Charles, 7, 17
Darragh, John, 7, 17
Darragh, Lydia, 7-17
Darragh, William, 7, 9, 17
David, Jozka, 182
Davis, Jefferson, 19, 22
"Denise" (Andrée Borrel), 124, 128,
    139
Dickinson, Lee Taylor, 102, 109
Dickinson, Velvalee, 101-114, 148
Driver, Joan, 157
Drtina, Dr. Prokop, 181, 183
Dubois, Alice (Louise Marie Jeanne
    Henriette de Bettignies), 46-73

Duel of Wits (Churchill), 142
Dufour, Jacques, 120-121
Duke, Col. Basil, 39
Dumba, Dr. Constantin, 78
Dzban, Jan, 191

Early, Jubal, 26, 29
Echo de Paris, l', 73
Eddy, Mary Baker, 123
Edmonds, Sarah Emma, 19
Edwards, Mena, 79
Eisenhower, Dwight D., 142, 161

Farragut, Admiral David, 26
Faye, Col. Lucien, 126
Fifth Avenue Association of New
    York, 76
First Aid Nursing Yoemanry, 119
Flora, 34, 38, 40
Foch, Marshal Ferdinand, 69
Forrest, Gen. Nathan Bedford, 30
Frank, Karl Hermann, 174, 177-178
Franz Ferdinand, Archduke, 47
"Fraulein Doktor," 51
Friends Society, 17

"Gaby," 130-132
Gates, Gen. Horatio, 4
Gebsottel, Gen. von, 53
George III, King of England, 4
Geyter, Elise de, 55, 64
Geyter, Georges de, 54-55
Gillem, Gen. Alvan C., 30, 36-41
Gmeiner, Joesph, 127-128
Goltz, Horst von der, 81
Gordon, Martha, see Heldt, Martha
Gottwald, Klement, 180-186, 189
Grandprez, Elise, 70
Grant, Ulysses, 24, 26
Granville, Christine, 133
Granville, Lord, 23
"Green Devils," 54
Greene, Gen. Nathaniel, 5
Greenhow, Rose O'Neal, 21-23, 24,
    84

Gregory, T. W., 76-78
Greyhound (ship), 20
Grouse, Pauline, 157

Hacha, Emil, 173-175, 178
Hague Convention, 117
Hale, Nathan, 3
Hallowes, Geoffrey, 136
Hampshire, HMS, 86
Hardinge, Ensign James, 20
Hart, Nancy, 23-24
Hawkins, Lt. "X," 39
Heidrich, Arnost, 174, 180, 184-185
Heldt, Martha, 79
Henlein, Konrad, 171, 174
Herzog, Anna, *see* Werner, Anna
Heydrich, Reinhard, 174
Himmel, Capt. Hermann, 53, 54, 59, 64, 66
Himmler, Heinrich, 128
Hitler, Adolf, 80, 168, 169, 170
Hofmann, Johanna, 146
Hollard, Michel, 156-157
Honeyman, John, 3
Horak, Bohuslav, 167, 172, 176
Horakova, Milada, 164-192
Horn, Werner, 81
Housatonic (ship), 88
Houtte, Marie Leonie van, 53, 64, 65, 68, 71, 73
Howe, Adm. Richard, 16
Howe, Sir William, 4, 5, 7, 10, 12-16
Huss, John, 190

Igel, Wolf von, 82
"Isabelle," 133

Jackson, Stonewall, 19, 23
"Jacqueline" (Yvonne Rudellat), 116-117, 133
Jacquet, Eugene, 60, 68, 71
"Jeanne Marie," *see* Khan, Noor Inayat
Jerushkova, Mila, 83-84
Jina, Dr., 188

Jockl, Director, 175
Johnson, Andrew, 29, 41
Johnson, Lt. John G., 42
Jonzen, Diana, 157
Jordan, Jesse, 145-146
Jules, 74

Kaltschmidt, Albert, 82
Kendall, Douglas, 157
Kennedy, Joseph B., 149
Kent, Taylor Gatewood, 147-149
Khan, Noor Inayat, 123-132, 134
Kieffer, Joseph, 125, 127-128, 133
Kiscox, Gertrude Blount, 150
Kitchener, Lord, 86
Kluck, Gen. Alexander von, 45
Koolbergen, Johann H. von, 82
Kral, Cenek, 165
Kretschmann, Baron Hans von, 85
Kretschmann, Baroness, *see* Victorica, Maria de
Kretschmann, Baroness Jennie von, 85
Kreutzinger, Wanda, 83

Ladies' Home Journal, 78
Lafayette, Marquis de, 5
Lavigne, Madeleine, 133
Leady, James, 41
Lee, Gen. Robert E., 29
Lefort, Cecily, 124, 128n.
Leigh, Vera, 128-129
Leonhardt, Emma Elise, 110
Leroux, Max, 74
Leveugle, Elise-Julie, 62, 66
Lew, Elizabeth van, 24
Libre Belgigue, La, 55
Liewer, Philip, 119-120
Lipp, Harriet, *see* Thompson, Harriet
"Lise," *see* Sansom, Odette Marie
Literary Digest, 75-76
Lopez, de Molinali, Inez, 101, 105, 107

"Louise" (Violette Szabo), 117-123, 132, 139
Louisville (ship), 167
"Loxley House," 7
Lusitania (ship), 77

McClellan, Gen. William B., 22
McDowell, Gen. Irvin, 21
McLane, Capt. Allen, 10, 13
McNally, James B., 112
"Madeleine," *see* Khan, Noor Inayat
Mapplebeck, Lt. Cyril, 60
Margaret, Vara, 83
"Marie" (Pearl Witherington), 136-138
"Martine," 130-132
Masaryk, Alice, 168
Masaryk, Jan, 182
Masaryk, Thomas G., 168, 169, 171
Mason, James, 126
Mata Hari, 70-71, 93, 132
Mauduit, Countess Roberta de, 141
Miller, Shackelford, Jr., 113
Moinet, Edward J., 110
Moog, Katie, 146
Morgan, Col. Daniel, 14, 15
Morgan, Gen. John Hunt, 26-40, 42, 43
Morgan, Martha, 28, 29
Morris, Maj. Joseph, 14
Morris, Ora Lipp, 44
"Mot du Soldat, Le," 66
My Imprisonment and The First Year of Abolition Rule at Washington (Greenhow), 23

"Nadine," 122
Nakashima, Kaoru, 103
Napoleon III, Emperor of the French, 23
New York *Times*, 77
New York *Tribune*, 75
Nicolai, Col. Walther, 53, 85, 86, 97
Niven, David, 126
Nix, Elizabeth Charlotte, 93

Noor, *see* Khan, Noor Inayat
Norman, Gilbert, 124, 132

"Odette," 138-139
O'Grady, Dorothy Pamela, 143-145
Oiseau de France, l', 55
Olchanesky, Sonia, 129
Old Capitol Prison, 20, 22
"On Your Guard Movement," 76

Papen, Capt. Franz von, 78-80
Patton, Gen. George, 177
"Paulette" (Diana Rowden), 124, 128
Pelantova, Rose, 168-170, 186
Peska, Dr. Zdanek, 169
Petit, Gabrielle, 66-69
Pinkerton, Allen E., 22
Plaminkova, Frantiska, 167, 175
Plewman, Elaine, 130-132, 134
Postal Telegraph Company, 83
"Prosper" (Francis Suttill), 124, 132
Providence *Journal*, 76
Provoust, Paul, 61

Rammeloo, Leonia, 70
"Raoul" (Peter Churchill), 133-136, 142
Ravensbruck, 122
Red Cross, 46, 48, 72
Reiswitz, Karl von, 82
Rintelen, Capt. Franz von, 80-81, 83, 91
Rodiger, Carl, 86-87, 95-96
Rohde, Werner, 129
Rolfe, Lillian, 122, 139
Rommel, Gen. Erwin, 118
Roosevelt, Eleanor, 190
Rosecrans, Gen. William S., 25
Rowden, Diana, 124, 128
Rude Pravo, 182, 183, 188, 189
Rudellat, Yvonne, 116-117, 133
Rumbaugh, Jenny, 29, 37

St. Gilles Prison, 66-68

Sanders, Gen. Liman von, 79
Sandys, Duncan, 155, 162
Sans Peur (yacht), 124
Sansom, Odette Marie, 133-136
Schattemann, Emilie, 70
Scheer, Adm. Reinhard von, 49-50
Schlieffen, Gen. Count von, 46
Scott, Samuel, 41
Secret Ink Bureau, 89
Shaine, Maurice, 112
Shaw (ship), 107
Sheridan, Gen. Philip, 26
Sherman, Gen. William Tecumseh, 26, 29
Shippen, Peggy, 16
Sigismund, Emperor, 190
"Simone" (Vera Leigh), 128-129
Sinn Feiners, 86
Skarbek, Countess Krystyn Gizycka, 133
Slade, Barbara, 151-163
Slansky, Rudolf, 191
Smith, Peggy, 141
Southgate, Maurice, 137
Spurna, Anezka Hodinova, 179
Stalin, Josef, 191
Stanton, Edwin M., 20, 23
Starr, Capt. John, 126
Stoeber, Dr., 65, 67-68
Storch, Despina Davidovich, 92-93
Sühren, Fritz, 134
Sullivan, Gen. John, 5
Sullivan, Margaret, 92
Suttill, Francis, 124, 132
Sykora, Dr. Vaclav, 187
Sylvestre, 74
Syracuse Herald, 76
Szabo, Etienne, 119
Szabo, Tania, 119, 123
Szabo, Violette, 117-123, 132, 139

Tallmadge, Maj. Benjamin, 13-16
Tapp, Ann, 157
Tellier, Louise, 68
Thompson, Harriet, 32, 40

Thompson, Lilly, 32, 40
Thompson, Sarah, 26, 31-44, 45, 118
Thompson, Sylvanis, 31-32
Thuliez, Louise, 64
Thwaites, Madeleine, 154-155
Tillman, Senator Benjamin R. "Pitchfork Ben," 75
Tolstoy, Leo, 123
Toulon, Association of Political Prisoners of, 73
Trotobas, Michel, 74
Trulin, Leon, 59, 68

United Veterans Association of France, 73

Victoria, Queen of England, 23
Victorica, José de, 85
Victorica, Maria de, 84-98
"Violette," 133
Vussiere, Marie de, *see* Victorica, Maria de

Wakasugi, Kaname, 104
Wake, Nancy, 141
Wallace, Mary, 105-108
Walsingham, Sir Francis, 3
Washington, George, 3-16
Wavell, Claude "Bill," 154
"Way the Spy Works, The," 78
Werner, Anna, 82-83
Wessels, Lt. Cdr. Herman, *see* Rodiger, Carl
Wheeler, Allen H., 163
"White Lady, The," 70
"White Rabbit," 122
Wilhelm II, German Kaiser, 45, 60, 69, 70, 76, 92
Williams, Dr. Alexander, 29
Williams, Catharine, 29, 37
Williams, Fanny, 29, 37
Williams, Joe, 29, 41
Williams, Lucy, 29-31, 41
Willot, Joseph, 54-55
Wilson, Woodrow, 70

Witherington, Pearl, 136-138
Wolkoff, Anna, 146-150
Women's Relief Corps of The Grand Army of the Republic, 26, 43
Women's Transport Service, 119
World War I, 45-98
World War II, 115-177

Yardley, Herbert O., 89
Yeo-Thomas, Wing Commander

Forest Frederick, 122
Yokoyama, Ichira, 104
"Yolande," 74
"Yvonne," 131-132

Zelle-better, Margarete (Mata Hari), 70-71, 93, 132
Zenkl, Dr. Petr, 168, 179, 180, 182, 183, 186
Zollner, Baroness Iona, 82